D0460581

SAINT AUGUSTINE

Early Church Father

Rachael M. Phillips

BARBOUR BOOKS

An Imprint of Barbour Publishing, Inc.

Other books in the "Heroes of the Faith" series:

Brother Andrew	George Müller
Gladys Aylward	Watchman Nee
Dietrich Bonhoeffer	John Newton
William and Catherine Booth	Florence Nightingale
John Bunyan	Luis Palau
John Calvin	Francis and Edith Schaeffer
William Carey	Charles Sheldon
Amy Carmichael	Mary Slessor
George Washington Carver	Charles Spurgeon
Fanny Crosby	John and Betty Stam
Frederick Douglass	Billy Sunday
Jonathan Edwards	Hudson Taylor
Jim Elliot	William Tyndale
Charles Finney	Corrie ten Boom
Billy Graham	Mother Teresa
C. S. Lewis	Sojourner Truth
Eric Liddell	John Wesley
David Livingstone	George Whitefield
Martin Luther	William Wilberforce
D. L. Moody	John Wycliffe
Samuel Morris	Some Gave All

© 2002 by Barbour Publishing, Inc.

ISBN 1-58660-574-7

All rights reserved. No part of this publication may be reproduced or transmitted in any form or by any means without written permission of the publisher.

Scripture quotations used by the author are taken from The King James Version of the Bible.

Published by Barbour Books, an imprint of Barbour Publishing, Inc., P.O. Box 719, Uhrichsville, OH 44683, www.barbourbooks.com

Cover illustration © Dick Bobnick.

Member of the
Evangelical Christian
Publishers Association

Printed in the United States of America.
5 4 3 2 1

SAINT AUGUSTINE

one

U nder no circumstances are you to inform my mother of our arrangement," said Augustine as he passed a small purse of coins to the innkeeper.

A greedy gleam sparkled in the man's black eyes, but he made a courteous bow and answered, "As you wish, young teacher."

Augustine nodded and paused at the door of the cramped room, searching the courtyard worriedly from behind a heavy curtain. *Surely Mother has not finished her afternoon prayers already,* he thought. He needed to complete some business matters and speak once more with the captain of their ship before meeting Monica for the evening meal. The heavy sweetness of the flowers, the heat of the North African afternoon that usually warmed him into drowsiness only sharpened his anxiety.

Ah, there she is! Monica knelt in the shade of an olive tree, her proud head bowed low under her favorite deep blue veil. Her lips moved in silent, earnest prayer, and a tear trickled down her cheek. For the thousandth time, Augustine felt guilt spread through him like a plague. But he took great satisfaction in the intensity of her supplications. Augustine's mother was praying he would remain in North Africa, and those petitions would no doubt occupy her for the rest of the afternoon.

Augustine slipped into a dark hallway and out the front door of the inn into the blinding sunlight. He hurried toward the great circular harbor of Carthage, where a ship would soon carry him away from his ignorant, rowdy students, away from a provincial career that would stifle his natural genius, away from a culture with only limited means of satisfying his hungry mind—and best of all, away from his mother, who had dogged his steps with her stubborn, passionate Christian faith since his birth.

"We must leave for Italy with the first rays of the sun," growled the burly, sun-blackened captain in a local Berber dialect. "There will be three of you?"

"Yes," answered Augustine. "Myself, my woman, and my son—he is almost eleven years old." A note of pride crept into his voice. Adeodatus, as his name denoted, was truly "given by God."

"It is good. We make no room for babies, howling little beasts who die of the fever before we leave the harbor." The captain grasped Augustine's money and slipped it into his coarse cape. "But be forewarned. If you are not on the ship before dawn, we will depart without you."

The ship's pilot had seen these soft sons of minor North African officials before. Latin-speakers, classically educated to the point they grew discontent in their native land, they became obsessed with dreams of Italy and its grandeur, sure of their welcome in the chief cities of the western Roman Empire. And this teacher had graced his palm with only a modest bribe, even though he was a highly visible

Manichaean, whose radical beliefs made Carthage some-what unsafe for him and his family. *Young fool!* The captain spat on the earthen floor of the smoky, oil-lit tavern.

"We will be there," said Augustine firmly, "although your ship cannot be said to be worth its outrageous price." He stared, cold and unblinking, at the man.

The sea captain fidgeted, then gulped the last of his drink and swore. "Be sure you are." His glance of grudging respect followed Augustine as he shoved his way through the crowded, evil-smelling room out into the narrow, dirty street.

"Your mother is still at her prayers," said Augustine's concubine when he returned to the inn.

"Good," said Augustine. "All is ready for our departure."

"I, too, have prepared everything." The woman bowed her head slightly in a gesture of respect, then paused, a ray of dying sunshine from the window caressing her glossy black hair. "I have not told the boy, as you wished," she said, "but he seems aware something is afoot."

Augustine grinned, then winced. "Of course he is aware of it! He is too much like his grandmother. If only Mother had not followed us here! As usual, she seems to know something is amiss. I hope her dreams do not disclose our plans." Monica occasionally had dreams about family members that revealed their secrets or predicted their futures with uncanny accuracy. "I'll speak with Adeodatus before we eat so he does not blurt out his suspicions to Mother." He knew he would find his son at the marketplace only a few blocks away, where he had played with other boys on earlier visits to the nearby chapel of Saint Cyprian and the seashore. Augustine touched the woman's curved, tawny cheek and left.

She watched his broad, strong back and erect carriage as he strode away. Faithful to Augustine since their teens, a doting mother to their son, whom she raised as a devout Christian, she would forever remain unnamed in Augustine's writings. As a social inferior, she knew only too well how rarely gentlemen kept their mistresses for a lifetime. But for now, he planned to take her with him to Italy, or he would never have disclosed his plans to leave. A slight chuckle escaped her full lips. Perhaps if they escaped the old one, Augustine might retain her, even if he married the aristocratic heiress who fit his ambitious plans better than she did. At any rate, she would play the docile servant and help Monica with the evening meal, as his mother always insisted on preparing Augustine's meals whenever she could. As fit her position, Augustine's concubine would pretend to know nothing.

After twelve years, she was adept at her role.

"Please, Augustine, return to Thagaste with me," pleaded Monica. "Carthage has done little for you these past seven years. Your students often refuse to pay your fees. Your father's house is honored in Thagaste; no one there would dare treat you with such discourtesy. And your brother could use your help managing your father's estate."

Augustine wiped his mouth and then slowly washed his hands in the basin his mother brought him. "Father's property is hardly big enough that Navigius needs my help. He always was the best administrator in the family. And if he needs more assistance, he can get it from Perpetua. How can you doubt my sister's abilities?" Augustine looked up from his hands and smiled. "After all, she learned everything she knows from you."

Monica tried to brush aside his compliment with a disapproving stare but found herself forced to settle for a halfhearted sigh. Perpetua was not the only one in the family who had learned the art of managing people and property from her.

"By the way, the lamb tasted superb, Mother. As always."

"It was wonderful, Grandmother!" echoed Adeodatus. He, like his father, had learned early that Monica melted under compliments about her cooking. Now he hoped for an extra sweet to take with him as he returned to his mother.

Adeodatus was not disappointed, as Monica deposited his favorite honey cake into his hand. He hugged her suddenly—a rarity, as the boy was generally too active for many embraces.

A rich smile lit Monica's face, and Augustine realized anew his mother still retained much of her youthful beauty. "Adeodatus, take care that you and your father meet me tomorrow morning for prayers at the chapel of Saint Cyprian."

"We will," said Augustine hastily, and Adeodatus dashed out the door to rejoin his friends.

"If you go to Rome," she said quietly, "I do not know if I shall ever see my grandson again." Her brown eyes softened, their fire extinguished by her tears.

Augustine shifted uncomfortably. "I have not yet decided which course I will pursue, Mother. There are advantages to both alternatives."

"What alternatives? Going to Rome or to Thagaste?"

"No, Mother." Augustine quietly insisted. "The alternatives consist of going to Rome or staying in Carthage. Thagaste is no place for a professor of rhetoric."

How could he make her understand? Thagaste, their hometown, had existed for three hundred years and it did have important connections to the rest of the Roman Empire. The North African provinces of the empire had long been an important source of food. The production and transport of grain and other agricultural products had made many transplanted Romans as well as "romanized" North Africans rich and provided many more with a comfortable lifestyle.

9

Augustine's father, Patricius, was not especially prosperous, but he had been a member of the town council, with duties as a tax collector. He was also a property owner, a mark of distinction in any farming community. Augustine grew up in a world defined and held secure by the wealth of Rome. The society he was born into admired the great orators, thinkers, political leaders, and military strategists who had shaped Roman culture for hundreds of years. They enjoyed Roman food, fashion, and entertainment. When they spoke with one another either to conduct business or to communicate with friends and family members, they were more likely to use Latin than any of the historic dialects of North Africa.

Trade with the rest of the empire paid for thousands of miles of carefully designed and meticulously maintained roads and bridges that could carry traffic quickly and easily in all kinds of weather. Those same roads allowed the armies of Rome to patrol the agricultural lands of North Africa and maintain a line of fortified outposts south of Thagaste, just beyond the Aures Mountains, which extended the empire's influence to the very edge of the great desert.

But in spite of all these advantages, Augustine's hometown was still a small, isolated rural community. It was located sixty miles inland from the Mediterranean coast, and those who wished to reach it faced a several days' journey over the Medjerda Mountains. Thagaste could never offer him the large arena he craved for displaying his intellectual and rhetorical gifts. What was his mother thinking! At least Carthage was a sizable port city, located right on the Mediterranean, with direct access to the commercial, political, and academic centers of the empire. If Augustine yielded to her pressure and returned to the place of his birth, he would give up any hope of advancing in his field.

His mother's voice broke into his thoughts. "With your

ability and reputation, you could make Thagaste a center of rhetoric if you returned," she insisted.

Augustine shook his head, smiling. "You far overestimate my influence, Mother. Besides, I long to teach pupils who actually enjoy learning. I've had my fill of spoiled youths who disrupt my classes and intimidate the younger students. And I've heard Rome is full of serious students, all of them committed to preparing themselves for important government careers. Alypius says so, and he's been in Rome for months. He's been meeting important people and has even managed to establish himself in the royal court."

Alypius had been an important part of his life for as long as Augustine could remember, and not just because he was related to Augustine's family. As children, they had hunted together in the fertile fields around Thagaste, climbed the majestic mountains near their town, tricked their schoolmaster when their studies bored them. Later, Augustine had taught Alypius for a time in Carthage and converted him to Manichaeanism, a controversial system of beliefs that distorted the basic teachings of the orthodox Christian church. Now his best friend was studying law in Rome and serving as an aide to the controller of funds within the imperial government. His letters only increased Augustine's resolve to try his wings in Italy.

"You are going to base your entire life's direction on Alypius's boastful letters?"

"Symmachus is now prefect of the city of Rome, Mother." *Not everyone,* Augustine thought smugly, *could claim the friendship of a Roman senator.* Symmachus had earlier held the temporary position of proconsul in Carthage. He'd soon heard of the brilliant young scholar Augustine, whose expertise in literature and rhetoric far surpassed his own. If Augustine could rekindle their friendship in Rome, his career would advance by leaps and bounds. "Perhaps he will give me letters of introduction to his cousin Ambrose in Milan," said Augustine.

Such a possibility silenced Monica for a moment as she considered the good that might result from a move to Rome and a later transfer to Milan. She had been praying for her son since his birth in 354. Was it possible that now, twenty-nine years later, God was drawing him along a path she had never considered? Augustine watched the thoughtful expression forming on his mother's face and knew he had gained the advantage in this particular round of their ongoing debate.

Milan had long been a prosperous center for trade because of its location at the heart of Rome's all-weather road system in northern Italy. As the threats from barbarian tribes north and east of the Alps increased during the fourth century, it also became a strategically important site for military leaders and the legions they commanded. By the second half of the fourth century, the emperors who ruled the western half of the empire were spending more and more time there, until Milan virtually replaced Rome as the center for the imperial court. Since 365 it had functioned as the capital of the entire western empire, and its population reached 130,000 to 150,000. The mix of bureaucrats, generals, aristocrats, merchants, soldiers, common people, and intellectuals of all kinds made it a wealthy and powerful city, just the sort of place where a young man might find almost unlimited opportunities to advance in his career.

As the population rapidly increased, Milan also had become an important stronghold for what people often called catholic or orthodox Christianity. The church had not yet divided into eastern and western branches, with eastern churches looking to the bishop of Constantinople for leadership and western churches looking to the bishop of Rome. Catholic or orthodox Christians throughout the Roman Empire proclaimed and defended the orthodox faith, drawn directly from the life and teachings of Jesus and the teachings of the apostles, contained in the books of the New Testament.

The most important leader of the church was Ambrose, the powerful bishop of Milan, who had been appointed to his position in 374 and was now famous throughout the empire for his thoughtfulness, his skill as an orator, and his fervent Christian piety. If Augustine's dreams of becoming a wealthy and influential scholar led him to Milan, Monica could pray that contact with Ambrose would influence her son to return to the biblical foundations of his faith and give up the philosophical nonsense of his Manichaean beliefs.

"If God should so will," Monica said slowly, "I would not forbid your going to Italy. The good He wishes for you, I do, also." Augustine felt himself quiver under her long look of yearning. His own eyes began to moisten.

His mother clasped him without speaking, then cleared the dishes away briskly as she began to plan aloud. "I will accompany you, of course, if you go, even though traveling is difficult. My bones grow old and tired!" Monica paused. "But Adeodatus needs me; that woman is no proper mother for such a child. Neither is she good for you."

Hot blood surged into Augustine's cheeks, throbbed in his temples. Ashamed because Manichaeans were to celebrate the pleasures of the spirit, not the body, he occasionally admitted to himself that he should not keep a concubine. But Augustine had resented his mother's repeated warnings about women since he was a child, and he took offense at her regular interference in his household. Twenty-nine years was long enough! How wonderful it would be to escape Monica's eternal nagging.

"I have not yet made a decision, Mother," he said carefully and with great dignity in order to hide his anger. "My friend Martius arrives at this inn within a day or so to prepare for his own voyage to Italy and to wait for favorable winds. I will then choose whether to accompany him or not."

"May he never come to tempt you to such folly!" An exasperated Monica swept from the room.

Have no fear, Mother, he will not come here. Augustine watched her retreating back and could not suppress a wicked smile. Martius, was, of course, the product of his own scheming imagination.

Aboard at last! Augustine inhaled the sea air, pleading with the placid predawn breezes. *Blow, blow, oh wind. Carry me far away to Italy, to life.*

Adeodatus huddled close beside him along the side of the ship, determined to remain awake, although they had stolen away from the inn not long after midnight. The boy had loved the clandestine escape through dark, silent streets and the shadowy rendezvous with the harbor men who loaded their baggage into small boats that rose and fell with the early morning tide as they made their way to the ship. Adeodatus knew Grandmother disapproved of the adventure his father wanted so much. But she was old, and what could you expect of old grandmothers?

"It may be hours before the breeze picks up," said his father. "Don't you want to go below to rest with your mother? I will awaken you when we leave the harbor."

Adeodatus shook his head. He wanted to watch everything, especially now that the slowly growing light made more activity aboard the ship visible. As the captain barked orders, the wiry, bronzed sailors climbed the rigging and adjusted the sails. The vessel was loaded to capacity with both grain and passengers, and it made its way slowly toward the wide passageway that connected the doughnut-shaped northern harbor of Carthage to the sea. Swells from the incoming tide rocked the ship like a friendly giant's hand.

Augustine clasped his son's shoulder. He remembered the joy of leaving backward Thagaste as a youth of twelve to study in Madauros and the intoxication of his early career in Carthage. But nothing in his past compared to this! Although his stomach lurched a little, his spirits rose with the wind. The offshore breezes seemed just as eager as he to leave the confines of North Africa. Whatever else the year 383 might bring, he was sure it would be a year of destiny, the beginning of a new adventure. *Blow, blow, carry me far away to Italy, to life.*

The stars retreated as the sky faded from black to gentle gray. Rosy streaks announced the sun's imminent arrival. The sails shivered, then ballooned as the breeze grew stronger. The captain smiled and called out new commands. The ship wallowed slightly as it crept down the canal and crossed the choppy water, marking the edge of the open sea.

Augustine glanced triumphantly at his son, but Adeodatus's eyelids had drifted shut, and the boy stood in a stupor. His father gently lowered him to the deck, covering him with his cloak.

"I'll try to wake you before we leave sight of land," Augustine murmured to the slumbering boy. "But knowing how deeply you sleep, you probably won't even remember!"

He straightened, stiffening. Did he spy a small, familiar figure on shore? Augustine stared, aghast, then shook himself. Why should his eyes have been drawn to this one person, when so many others stood along the cluttered seaside? The rising sun highlighted a splash of blue on the figure as it moved quickly toward the very edge of the water. He muttered a curse under his breath and tore unwilling eyes away from the shore. Moving to the other side of the vessel, Augustine peered at the smooth, empty horizon that beckoned to him. *Come, Augustine, come to freedom, fame and fortune. Come to Italy.*

He did not look back.

"Where is Augustine?" Monica demanded of the timid young woman who had waited on her son's family. "Where is he? When did he leave? He and my grandson were to join me at Saint Cyprian's for morning prayers." The girl dropped to her knees and cowered before the older woman but remained silent. Augustine's mother turned from her in disgust and loudly demanded answers to the same questions from every servant she met. After several minutes, the innkeeper appeared, pleading with her to remain calm.

"Calm? Calm? My son Augustine and his family have disappeared! When did they leave? Were they all right? Did they speak with you?" Monica was usually known for her dignified behavior, but now she raged like a mother bear deprived of her cubs.

The innkeeper recognized danger in her flashing eyes. "Yes, Mistress, the young teacher and his family were in good health when they left during the night. I am not sure where they went," he said smoothly, "but I thought I heard the child mention sailing on a ship."

"Which one? *Which?*"

"I have no idea, Mistress. They took all their belongings with them." *They also paid me well,* he added silently, *but I doubt if you will be able to overtake them to discuss that fact.*

Without another word, Monica stormed out the front door of the inn. Anger and inconsolable grief fought within her as she wiped her streaming eyes and ran through the now-busy streets of Carthage toward the harbor. Panting, she questioned every harbor hand she encountered until she found the boatmen who had transported Augustine, his concubine, and Adeodatus.

"Yes, Mistress, we carried that family out to Captain Zama's ship. No, Mistress, the winds rose during the night, and the ship departed two, maybe three hours ago."

O Lord, could You not have stilled the winds as You did on the Sea of Galilee? Did You take my children away from me? Monica hurried along the ship canal until it reached the open sea. She stumbled toward the beach and lay prostrate in the hot sun for many hours, digging her fingers into the sand, weeping and praying. *If only I could be sure Augustine will find his way back to You, O Lord. Rome is full of idols, heresies, evil. . . . And he, in his quest for wisdom, is like a child who plays under the hooves of a rearing horse. . . .*

Beyond the reach of Monica's despair, Augustine was still drinking in the wildness and wonder of his first sea voyage to Italy. He had no idea his flight from North Africa would only serve to put him back on the road to his mother's God.

Years later, he would remember both her pain and the mysterious faithfulness of God in a prayer: "What was it, O Lord, that she was asking of thee in such a flood of tears but that thou wouldst not allow me to sail? But thou, taking thy own secret counsel and noting the real point to her desire, didst not grant what she was then asking in order to grant to her the thing that she had always been asking. The wind blew and filled our sails, and the shore dropped out of sight. Wild with grief, she was there the next morning and filled thy ears with complaints and groans which thou didst disregard. . . . She loved to have me with her, and did not know what joy thou wast preparing for her through my going away."[1]

two

A ugustine lay on his pallet, his very bones throbbing with pain. He did not dare sit up, as his tyrannical stomach hardly allowed him to breathe, let alone move so much.

His concubine gently wiped his hot forehead with a cool, damp cloth. He snapped at her: "Leave me in peace! I'd rather die alone than be surrounded by idiots!"

She left with a backward glance of mingled pity and scorn. During their voyage, Augustine had discovered the sea did not agree with him. He had spent most of the journey below deck, groaning with nausea. She and Adeodatus, after initial seasickness, had enjoyed the rolling majesty and cool spray of the Mediterranean and the brilliant joy of sunny, hot days on board ship. She thought their arrival in Italy would help him forget the miserable crossing to Italy, which had left him pale and weak from lack of food. Instead, some new illness had assailed him and now refused to leave, even though they had paid a North African doctor exorbitant fees for a healing amulet.

Augustine gritted his teeth and tried to calm himself.

Once, at age seven, while suffering through a serious illness, he had begged to be baptized in order to avoid the terrors of God's judgment. The idea was quickly abandoned, however, when he began to get better. Now, anger at this lingering illness was causing him more discomfort than any thoughts about death or the afterlife. The feeling that life was passing him by, that opportunities were being missed, burned more fiercely than the remnants of his fever. He must get better, he must! Day after day, he heard the fascinating sounds of Rome just outside his window. He yearned to breathe the city's air.

Not only did the life of an invalid bore Augustine beyond belief, but he must soon make contact with influential people who could send students his way, students whose wealthy, aristocratic relatives would eventually further his rhetorical career. He was a brilliant scholar, an eloquent speaker; yet here he lay, retching and sniveling like. . .like. . . some sick, useless old woman! Gallio, a fellow Manichaean, had generously opened his home to Augustine and his family with no mention of payment, but the young teacher needed to add to the funds inherited from his father's estate and now carefully hoarded to last as long as possible while he established himself.

Even if by magic Mother appeared in Rome, she would never give me more money.

When Monica had first discovered that her son had joined the heretical sect of Manichaeans, she had flatly refused him permission to enter her house and had relented only because of her bishop's advice and a dream that assured her of Augustine's eventual return to the orthodox faith.

He winced as he remembered his night escape from Carthage. *Her anger about my religious convictions might have subsided, but she still despises anyone who tricks her, especially if lying is involved. . . .*

19

A portrait of Monica's proud, strong face appeared unbidden in Augustine's mind. Her dark eyes stared at him, unblinking; the dreaded accusation radiated from them. *If only I could shake my head and be free of her!* But tears filled his eyes, too. He quickly squeezed them back.

He had feared his mother as a child because of her passionate opinions and determination to make him obey. But her tender touch spoke over and over again of the love she had for him. His mother always cherished him, even while sternly reprimanding him for ransacking her pantry to feed his many friends or playing truant from school. His father, Patricius, a pagan who was baptized shortly before his death, had taken pride in Augustine's precociousness and sacrificed to provide for his education; yet he had remained a distant, cold figure to the boy. But the light of Monica's love had filled Augustine's early life with warmth and color. It was just as real, just as much a part of his past as the golden aura of the African sun illuminating olive tree-covered hills and shimmering in the streets of Thagaste. Would he live to see Monica or Thagaste again?

Even as he fought back tears, Augustine smiled wryly. To think he, Aurelius Augustine, missed Thagaste!

From the time of his birth in 354 A.D., he and everyone else in his family had worked so that he could obtain some position from the imperial court that would take him far from his home in the province of Numidia. Though isolated, Thagaste looked nothing like the primitive little villages perched on the hills surrounding it. Built by the Romans three centuries before Augustine's birth, Thagaste boasted a carefully planned street system, luxurious public baths fed by an aqueduct, and an amphitheater almost as large as Rome's Colosseum. These contributions to the health, comfort, and status of the town had been donated over several generations by wealthy patrons. As with most Roman towns, Thagaste was designed to last. (Today Augustine's birthplace is called Souk Ahras and is located in Algeria). But by the time Augustine was growing up in this well-ordered society, signs of decay were visible everywhere. Rich landowners still lived near Thagaste on opulent rural estates, but their money provided wild animal and gladiator entertainments that riveted the local population's attention and discouraged them from demanding better living conditions.

We no longer prosper as we did in the past, thought Augustine. *The attacks of the barbarians have changed everything.* Roman emperors were now forced to spend enormous sums protecting their empire; monies for maintenance of far-flung provincial towns simply did not exist. It was difficult enough to find money to keep the roads repaired so that imperial troops could move quickly to block any attacks on those towns. The rich hoarded their resources, fearing the future. Broken statues went unrepaired; beautiful buildings slowly deteriorated. Augustine's hometown wore the weary look of a forgotten concubine.

If I had stayed in Thagaste, Augustine reflected, *I would have become like my father.* His shudder, for once, was not due to his sickness. Patricius had been a city official with a proper pedigree but little money. He managed to feed his household, which consisted of several relatives and slaves, as well as his wife and children, but Augustine remembered how shabbily his mother and sister sometimes dressed and how his education had placed a strain on the family finances.

Thank heaven for Romanianus, Augustine thought. If his wealthy benefactor had not taken interest in the budding genius of his young relative, Augustine would still be living in Thagaste—*probably running in the streets and tearing up the town as I did that year when I had to leave school in Madauros for lack of funds.* He remembered how he and his young friends had roamed the town late at night, looking for mischief. Finding a pear tree loaded with ripe but wormy fruit near Augustine's family vineyard, the gang stripped the branches and carried off their booty in triumph.

They tasted terrible! Augustine remembered how he had forced himself to eat one. *Those pears were so rank we threw them to the pigs. Why did I do such a thing?* Romanianus had given Augustine free access to his luxurious home and pantry; he could have eaten far more delectable fruit whenever he wished. *Fruit!* Augustine's stomach rumbled ominously. *I don't even want to think about it. . . .*

But Romanianus had provided the necessary funds the next year to send Augustine at age seventeen to Carthage, the intellectual center of the area, for his advanced education. Augustine had hated his early school years in Thagaste, where teachers used eight-hundred-year-old methods. His schoolmaster dissected a passage from classical Roman works of literature, such as those by Virgil or Cicero, then expected rote memorization by his students. Augustine liked those writings better than works in the Greek, because they were in his native Latin. As he grew older, he realized that writing and speaking captivated him like nothing else. But he suffered deeply when his teacher routinely caned him because he refused to learn Greek, which bored him even more than arithmetic.

Augustine had rejoiced as he impatiently kissed his mother good-bye and left Thagaste for a new life in Carthage. He never wanted to return. Freedom! Freedom! Even now, as he lay ill, Augustine could taste the joy of release from provincial narrowness to a city of culture and intellectual liberation. He had savored his freedom when he first arrived in Carthage. He would do so again in Rome, the center of the world.

"How are you this evening, Augustine? Have you rested well today?"

Augustine slowly turned over. The kind elderly eyes of his host, Gallio, warmed his weary heart. "Yes, Gallio. I even ate a little broth and feel strengthened by it. Perhaps I will eat more tomorrow."

"God grant it be so," said Gallio fervently. "Your face shows more color. It is evident someone's prayers prevail for you."

"I am sure my mother prays," agreed Augustine, "although she has no idea of my illness and is still incensed at my coming to Rome."

"She opposed your becoming a Manichaean, I suppose?" asked Gallio.

"Of course. She would not listen to my reasons!" Augustine's lips tightened.

"You must not upset yourself. Think no more of her anger but of her love. Rest, my friend."

Augustine nodded gratefully. Gallio slipped out as twilight began to drift into the room.

Augustine sighed. Gallio had welcomed him and his family with open arms, even though Augustine was a stranger and might very well have carried a plague into his house. They had enjoyed his hospitality for weeks. The Manichaeans regarded each other as family and provided for each other's needs. Augustine, who as a child made friendships which would last a lifetime, was drawn to their warmth.

But Mother was right, thought Augustine in frustration. *Although I want to believe Manichaeanism, I can no longer accept many of their ideas. Manichaeans believe good is one force and evil a separate force. If God is the good force and creates only good things, where does this evil come from? Manichaeans seem to believe the good remains passive while evil runs rampant. But where is the spiritual progress in that? And how does the good remain strong?*

Augustine tossed restlessly on his pallet. His mind still wrestled with the endless questions that had overwhelmed him since he first came to Carthage. Had it really been twelve years ago? Intoxicated with the sights and sounds of the city and the liberty to pursue the sexual love he had craved, Augustine spent his first year in frantic pursuit of pleasure. He grew addicted to the theater, especially scenes in which lovers were forced to separate. He loved attending gladiatorial games with his rowdy new friends, cheering madly with the rest of the bloodthirsty crowd as muscular, bronzed men slashed at each other with swords and pitted their wits and strength against bears and other wild animals. He met girls, often at church, and reveled in the sin his mother had strictly forbidden.

He marveled at the "Eversores," upperclassmen who enjoyed intimidating professors and first-year students and breaking up classes. While he longed for—and won—their acceptance, he secretly felt appalled by their behavior.

Carthage presented an exotic feast for a small-town boy, intellectually as well as sensually. Free from the floggings that discouraged rather than encouraged his eager mind, Augustine enjoyed the challenges presented by his pagan teachers.

During his second year Augustine had tired of the string of bruising, fickle love affairs that filled his days with ecstasy and anguish. He had taken his concubine then, a common practice among respectable young Romans who wanted to elevate their careers before seeking an advantageous marriage. The woman came from a class below him, of course; that was to be expected. They fought prodigiously but enjoyed meeting each other's needs, a situation which satisfied Augustine.

Although the church tolerated such arrangements, Mother, of course, disapproved. But I think she was vastly relieved the girl was Catholic and that I did not involve myself with a married woman. Then Adeodatus was born, and she could not contain her delight, although she tried to at first.

I was far from delighted but could not help watching my baby as he slept. Years later Augustine would remember that tender time and praise God for the beauty of his son: "O Lord my God, thou who gavest life to the infant, and a body which, as we see, thou hast furnished with senses, shaped with limbs, beautified with form, and endowed with all vital energies for its well-being and health—thou dost command me to praise thee for these things, to give thanks unto the Lord, and to sing praise unto his name, O Most High. . . . Thou alone who madest all things fair and didst order everything according to thy law."[1]

Now Augustine tried to see the evening star from his bed, as his Manichaean beliefs had taught him to seek light at all times. *Perhaps Adeodatus can visit me tomorrow.* He missed the boy's energy and bright, insightful questions.

When is she coming to light the lamps? Irritated, Augustine listened for his concubine's step. *I should have left her behind in Africa, as I did Mother. Here in Rome I will reap no advantages from my ties with such a woman. But then, Adeodatus still needs her.*

The room darkened, and Augustine's loneliness grew. Deep down he knew he needed her, too.

"It is time you stop lolling around at Gallio's and begin to make a name for yourself!"

Augustine gripped his friend's hand. Alypius pounded him on the back. The two North Africans were glad the Mediterranean Sea no longer separated them. Alypius's position as assistant controller of the royal treasury apparently agreed with him. *Alypius must be moving in aristocratic circles,* Augustine noted. *He has lost much of his accent, and see how he throws back his head!* Alypius wore clothes of excellent quality, as well as a new air of dignity foreign to their days in Carthage together.

"I suppose you are too high and mighty to remain friends with your old teacher from the provinces," Augustine said.

"Perhaps it is beneath me to be seen with you, but I am in a charitable mood. Do your students know you had to leave Carthage in the middle of the night to get away from your mother?"

"If you don't tell them, I won't inform the royal controller you were mistakenly dragged off to jail as a thief when you were a student."

"Thank you!" Alypius laughed and motioned toward the marketplace. "I still have nightmares about that horrible day! Let's find a good cup of wine and a place to talk." The two plunged into the crowds that always gathered on market days and found a bench where they could sit down.

"How are your students? Are they any more attentive than they were in Carthage?" asked Alypius.

Augustine winced. "Perhaps a little; it appears I was mistaken about their devotion to learning here in Rome. Marcus, Junius, and Gaius perform adequately. But Antonius and Menas make it their business to destroy any serious thinking we can accomplish. They are worse than the Carthaginians."

Alypius laughed. "At least they pay better here, or rather their fathers do."

"True. All of them appear to be from noble houses of substantial wealth. I should do well." Augustine frowned. "But it is far more expensive to teach here. I must maintain a classroom that befits a professor of rhetoric, and I have to pay a doorkeeper to admit my students for their appointments."

"Far more formal than the days in Carthage when we barged in and out of class at will!" Now it was Alypius's turn to frown. "Did you say Menas? One of my other professor friends mentioned a Menas who nearly drove him insane, then failed to pay him at the end of the term. Be wary, Augustine. A noble family does not insure a noble nature. Thieves abound here in Rome, both in poor and rich houses."

"I will be careful," Augustine answered, touched at his friend's concern. They went on to speak of friends and relatives in Thagaste and Carthage, laughing and joking, oblivious to the noise around them. As they talked, the years fell away. Augustine saw once more the earnest youth Alypius, who had attached himself to Augustine, the budding professor. He was one of the first to welcome Augustine's new religious ideas and adopt them as his own.

Did I mislead you, Alypius? Have I guided you into a Manichaean maze where we will never find true wisdom?

The quest for true wisdom had drawn the young Augustine like the fragrance of his mother's honey cakes. One of his professors had assigned the Roman author Cicero's *Hortensius*; dutifully Augustine had begun reading, only to be electrified by the pagan writer's admonition that a philosopher must be "enkindled and inflamed to love, to seek, to obtain, to hold, and to embrace, not this or that sect, but wisdom itself, wherever it might be."[2] *Hortensius* transformed his entire world: "Now it was this book which quite definitely changed my whole attitude and turned my prayers toward thee, O Lord, and gave me new hope and new desires.[3] How ardent was I then, my God, how ardent to fly from earthly things to thee!"[4]

Augustine had initially studied the Scriptures eagerly, as his mother's faith had had an effect on him. ("And whatsoever was lacking that name [Christ], no matter how erudite, polished, and truthful, did not quite take complete hold of me,"[5] he later wrote.) But Augustine had met with keen disappointment. The narrative of the Bible did not compare to the artistry and distinction of Cicero's writing, he felt. The Old Testament particularly disturbed him, with its barbaric descriptions of killing and animal sacrifices and its often frightening picture of the wrathful Jehovah, who reminded him too much of his father.

He began to listen to the effective speeches and debates of the Manichaean leaders, who claimed to possess a purer, more educated view of Christianity. To a Manichaean, Christ was completely spiritual; he certainly was not born as a human and only appeared to agonize on the cross and die. Mani, who founded the Mesopotamian sect around 244 A.D., had considered himself the Holy Spirit. The Elect, or high leaders of Manichaeanism, seemed holy and all-wise to Augustine, with their mystical ways, their celibacy, and constant fasting.

Augustine had become a Hearer, a disciple, who brought the Elect their food, as they were forbidden to kill any living thing, including plants. As such, he was subject to less stringent rules. He knew that sexual contact was physical and therefore vastly inferior to the spiritual Light, but he appreciated the Manichaean view that no believer was responsible for the vices he found in himself. Blame belonged to the Evil, the powerful impersonal force that made a constant assault on the Good. He could continue keeping his woman without too much argument with his conscience.

"Augustine! You are thinking again and haven't heard a word I've said!" Alypius poked him in the ribs. "At least, it's good to know some things don't change. You always did walk around in a fog."

"Merely because I found my own conversation far more intelligent than that of those around me."

"I should leave you to your own company, then, but it would not be good for you. You already bury yourself in your books and your work. After such an illness, you need time for relaxation and dining, so you can grow a large stomach like the rest of the bureaucrats."

"*You* certainly cannot claim moderation in your work. And you're thin as you were as a new student in Carthage."

"But not as thin as you are, Augustine. You are positively emaciated." Alypius's eyes were dark with anxiety.

Augustine laughed. "I am sure you have just the remedy for my malaise."

"Indeed, I do! Let's dine sumptuously, then go to the circus; my favorite gladiator fights today. He is something to see, Augustine."

Alypius's voice tightened; his eyes glittered with anticipation. Augustine searched his friend's face in alarm, but he tried to keep his voice casual. "I thought you had decided to stop going to the games for awhile."

Alypius shrugged impatiently. "I did. I didn't attend any at first. But some friends literally dragged me to one a few months ago, and it made our shows in Carthage seem as exciting as our arithmetic classes back in Thagaste." He pulled on Augustine's arm. "I've only gone a few times since then. It's nothing like Carthage, when I went constantly."

Augustine sighed. Alypius had been logical even as a child; even though he was younger than Augustine, he had proved a worthy opponent in their frequent debates. He also possessed a deep sense of integrity. Why did Alypius seem to lose all that when he became part of the cheering crowds at the gladiator shows? Augustine himself had never become addicted, as Alypius had in Carthage, but the battles between men and beasts, the excitement of the arenas, had always quickened his own pulse. And he was weary of teaching bored, restless students. "All right, Alypius. Perhaps I do need a little entertainment."

"I can't believe how much they want for this!" exclaimed Augustine as he felt for his nearly-flat purse. "Carthage was so much cheaper!"

"Please allow me," said Alypius, throwing coins at the attendant.

The two friends entered the Colosseum, finding their way to the level where minor aristocrats and officials were seated out of the blazing sun. Conversations hummed lazily; one matron near them exclaimed over the size of the leopards of the morning's *venatio,* in which less-skilled gladiators called *bestiarii* fought exotic wild beasts. Another deplored the fact that the executions, which were routinely conducted during lunchtime, were not finished before she returned from her meal. "Such spectacles are for the rabble," she complained, "not proper ladies and gentlemen."

Augustine, like most Romans, considered the public deaths of criminals appropriate as demonstrations of the empire's authority to exercise justice and protection for its people. Still, he had never enjoyed the sight of an unarmed condemned man trying to fend off the claws and fangs of a lion or bear. He knew, too, that before Emperor Constantine had become a Christian, many pious men and women like his mother had faced the wild beasts or had been crucified or burned at the stake for the entertainment of people like Alypius and himself who had paid well to see the spectacle.

"Here they come!" Alypius roared, and the thunderous crowd rose to greet the procession of gladiators, who raised their daggers and swords in greeting.

"Not a single slave fighter among them!" Alypius said excitedly. "We will see some of the best today!" Many professional gladiators were captured prisoners of war who battled three to five years in hopes of winning their liberty. But others were free Romans who chose the profession because of the high pay and benefits for themselves and their families, as well as the fame and glory it brought them. All professionals trained like athletes in schools sponsored by the government for the two or three fights a year that would mean life or death for them.

"There he is! That's Lucius! He fights last today because he's the best!" The massive man carried a small circular shield and a wicked-looking, curved Thracian sword. Other fighters also wore armor and weaponry reminiscent of Rome's enemies in the early days of the gladiatorial games: the Samnites with their plumed helmets and oval shields; a Gallic gladiator, or *murmillo,* who carried a rectangular shield and wore a visored helmet ornamented with fish, and the *retiarii,* who used nets and three-pronged spears as weapons.

Augustine cheered with the crowd when a gladiator made a powerful or dexterous move and voiced his displeasure when one eliminated his opponent almost immediately, as well-trained gladiators always extended the spectacle for the benefit of the crowd.

"Jugula! Jugula!" Alypius howled for blood. His eyes arrested Augustine's own cheering. Later he was to write of his friend's insanity produced by the games: "He did not

31

turn away, but fixed his eyes on the bloody pastime, unwittingly drinking in the madness—delighted with the wicked contest and drunk with blood lust. He was now no longer the same man who came in, but was one of the mob he came into, a true companion of those who had brought him. . . . He looked, he shouted. . .and he took away with him the madness that would stimulate him to come again: not only with those who first enticed him, but even without them; indeed, dragging in others besides."[6]

"Alypius! Let us go!" shouted Augustine into his friend's ear. "We have seen enough today." But Alypius, deaf to anything but the fight, watched Lucius skillfully battle the wiry blond Germanic warrior who was not as large as his opponent. Lucius's muscles rippled, his sweat shining in the brilliant heat of the afternoon and dripping to the parched ground. Augustine thought of the Greek hero Hercules. Could any god rival the terrible beauty of Lucius in combat?

But suddenly the smaller man leapt in, dagger moving like lightning, and wounded Lucius's arm so he could hardly grasp his own weapon. Lucius fought fiercely, valiantly, and managed to wound his opponent several times. But the loss of blood and the oven-like heat took its toll on the big man.

"Habet, hoc habet! He has had it!" yelled the mob.

Augustine stared at Alypius; daunted, at first, by his champion's imminent loss, he quieted momentarily. But several around them began to call for Lucius's death as the German pressed his advantage. Hundreds of others joined in the ugly chorus. To Augustine's horror, Alypius, too, began to scream with them. *Is he crying out for the death of a man he so admired only a few hours ago?*

When the German had finally fought Lucius to his knees, the exhausted gladiator raised his left forefinger, and the referee stopped the fight. The Colosseum shook with the roar of those who called for mercy in the face of his courage; others howled for his death. All eyes were fastened on the editor, a wealthy aristocrat who had sponsored the games that day in honor of his deceased brother. Would he grant Lucius, who had won many bouts, pardon for his failure?

Grimly, the white-haired man held out his thumb like the sharp point of a sword: death.

The panting Lucius slowly placed his hand on the victor's thigh, his face immobile. The German plunged his sword into Lucius's neck as the crowd yowled in frenzied approval.

Augustine dragged his friend from the Colosseum. Alypius, who as a junior magistrate had not hesitated to defy a powerful Senator who had offered him bribes; Alypius who did not battle an insatiable craving for sex, as Augustine did; Alypius, with his bright, rational mind and clear, cool judgments—how could this be the same man?

The Manichaean Elect say it is the evil force that does this to Alypius, Augustine mused, *just as it is the evil force that gives me no peace from my constant need for women.* Such a thought usually comforted him and eased his sense of responsibility. But now he shivered as he tried to calm his friend. Would the Evil conquer them both?

three

Y ou will be at the meeting on Monday?" Alypius asked anxiously. "It is the Bema, you know." The Bema was the most important of all Manichaean ceremonies; it commemorated the martyrdom of their founder, Mani, and involved the welcoming of new Hearers and members of the Elect.

"Of course, I'm going." Augustine could not hide his lack of enthusiasm. Gallio, who had become a close friend, was to become a member of the Elect at this Bema. He could own nothing and so would become an itinerant wanderer throughout the empire, a celibate follower of the Light who prayed seven times a day and fasted a quarter of the year. His wife would probably become one of the Elect, too. Such a thought depressed Augustine; Gallio's gentle, loving household would no longer exist. Their greedy eldest son, Horatio, would no doubt inherit most of his father's wealth. Horatio was as well-known for his meanness of spirit as his father was for his generosity but had dared mistreat his family and slaves only when Gallio was absent.

"You question the validity of the Manichaean belief."

It was a statement, not a question. Alypius had been Augustine's close friend for years; though Augustine was adept at fooling his Manichaean friends, he could not deceive Alypius. It was the first time, however, either of them had openly stated their doubts.

"I must think this through, Alypius," said Augustine.

"I know," said his friend. "But do not reach hasty conclusions. The Manichaeans have practiced their faith with all sincerity before us both. They made valuable contacts for me when I first came to Italy and now do the same for you."

"I know, I know," said Augustine irritably. New students had contacted him solely on the basis of the recommendations of his Manichaean friends. Opportunities to exhibit his rhetorical expertise multiplied because of the influence of their large community in Rome. And he owed his very life to Gallio's kindness. He stared at his feet and repeated, "I must think this through, Alypius."

"Yes, you must." Alypius put his arm around his downcast friend. "And I know you will make the right decision."

Augustine looked into his understanding eyes. *How glad I am to have a friend like you!*

"Speak with me about it when you have come to a conclusion," Alypius said and left Augustine to ponder.

Augustine continued to weigh the edicts of the religion he had accepted for nine years. As a twenty-year-old, Manichaeanism had seemed the answer to all his doubts about traditional Catholic Christianity. At first Augustine had feasted on the new precepts, which seemed to coincide perfectly with those of Cicero. He had amazed the intelligentsia of Carthage by conquering Aristotle's *Ten Categories,* a feat which rivaled those of the elite intellectuals in Rome. He had readily converted his friends in Carthage to Manichaeanism and built a large sphere of influence as he publicly debated Catholic Christians with less rhetorical ability who tried to oppose his Manichaean beliefs. When he returned to Thagaste to teach for a brief period, he even convinced his patron Romanianus of the truth of his Manichaean beliefs. His relatives had listened respectfully—all but his mother!

Most of Augustine's first contacts with Manichaeanism were educated Carthaginians who had rejected the "barbaric" aspects of Christianity as he had. But none of them answered his most pressing philosophical questions. As he continued in the sect, he increasingly encountered merchants, tradesmen, and other unschooled people who blindly accepted the tenets of the seven books of Manichaeanism. Augustine had read from those seven sacred books, which were intricately embellished with beautiful illustrations, but he was not prepared to accept all their wisdom, as he knew they flatly contradicted known facts about eclipses and the movement of the stars. Such a disparity had disturbed him greatly, as, above all, Augustine was interested in truth.

When he had posed his questions to his learned Manichaean friends, they had all assured him Faustus of Milevis would resolve all his doubts when he returned to Carthage from his current missionary journey.

His pamphlets use excellent logic and educated language, Augustine had thought. *The most intelligent Manichaeans regard him as the ultimate member of the Elect, the spiritual authority of North Africa. I'm sure he will open my eyes to the wisdom I am missing in reading the sacred books.* For years he had eagerly awaited the arrival of the saint.

When Faustus had come to Carthage in 383 A.D., his

36

fluid rhetorical style and gracious warmth had captured Augustine.

But as a lowly Hearer, thought Augustine, *I have no opportunity to share with him the questions in my heart. How can I confide my doubts when I am but one of our large assembly? I can't speak with him before or afterward because he is always surrounded by a gaggle of followers bringing him food and fawning on him.*

Augustine had summoned his courage and accosted Narcissus, the leader of the Elect in Carthage. "May a few friends and I meet privately with Faustus for an hour or so? We desire to learn as much as possible from the great master."

Narcissus had smiled at the young teacher's eagerness. He had celebrated Augustine's conversion to Manichaeanism and rejoiced in his growing influence on Carthaginian students and professors. *We must encourage Augustine in any way we can.* "Wait while I speak with Faustus," he'd said and returned a moment later to report happily, "Faustus will see you this evening with the rising of the moon." Narcissus had beamed. "A fitting time, when all of the scattered fragments of light liberated from God's people rise together to fill the moon and illuminate the night."

Augustine had nodded, thinking, *I hope Faustus's light will illuminate me.* He had tired of debating with himself, wrestling endlessly over astronomical calculations.

But when the little group met together, Augustine was astounded to find that Faustus actually possessed far less education than himself. "I laid before him some of my doubts. I discovered at once that he knew nothing of the liberal arts except grammar, and that only in an ordinary way."[1] "For as soon as it became plain to me that Faustus was ignorant in those arts in which I had believed him eminent, I began to despair of his being able to clarify and explain all these perplexities that troubled me. . . . Their books are full of long fables about the sky and the stars, the sun and the moon. . . . I had ceased to believe him able to show me in any satisfactory fashion what I so ardently desired: whether the explanations contained in the Manichaean books were better or at least as good as the mathematical explanations I had read elsewhere. But when I proposed that these subjects should be considered and discussed, he quite modestly did not dare to undertake the task, for he was aware that he had no knowledge of these things and was not ashamed to confess it. . . . Faustus had a heart which, if not right toward thee, was at least not altogether false toward himself; for he was not ignorant of his own ignorance."[2]

"Your questions did not worry him at all," Nebridius had said as the group walked home. "He seemed completely unconcerned as to whether he could answer them or not." Nebridius, whom Augustine later referred to as his "sweet friend,"[3] nevertheless disliked those who offered quick, unthinking answers to complicated problems. He did not know how to regard someone who offered none. Nebridius watched Augustine closely for his reaction.

"I don't know what to think." Augustine had shaken his head. *I admire those who do not pretend great knowledge they do not possess, but his ignorance appalls me! I didn't know whether to turn my back on Faustus forever or congratulate him on his modesty.* His thoughts swirled more than ever, and his stomach churned. "I am to meet with him again soon; Faustus seemed delighted that I teach literature and wants to discuss some works with which I am familiar."

Despite his turmoil, Augustine had enjoyed spending time with the Manichaean leader. He found Faustus a pleasant, brilliant conversationalist who stated and restated Manichaean dogma in innovative ways. But such tactics did not impress Augustine. "My ears had already had their fill of such stuff, and now it did not seem any better because it was better expressed nor more true because it was dressed up in rhetoric; nor could I think the man's soul necessarily wise because his face was comely and his language eloquent."[4] *A wine's quality,* thought Augustine stubbornly, *does not depend on the elegance of its server. I do not judge food by the richness of its dish. Nor shall I determine truth by the attractiveness of its supposed bearer.* Even as the two cultivated their friendship, Augustine's regard for Manichaeanism waned; he found himself tutoring the exalted leader of the Elect in literature!

Augustine's disappointment had fueled his desire to go to Rome later that year to continue his search for wisdom. But he had grown to love his Manichaean friends and was reluctant to lose their fellowship. And key points of their doctrine continued to appeal to him: He much preferred to blame his sin on a shadowy, impersonal Evil, rather than on himself.

"I loved to excuse my soul and accuse something else inside me (I knew not what) but which was not I. But, assuredly, it was I, and it was my impiety that had divided me against myself. That sin then was all the more incurable because I did not deem myself a sinner. It was an execrable iniquity, O God Omnipotent, that I would have preferred to have thee defeated in me, to my destruction, than to be defeated by thee to my salvation."[5]

In Rome Augustine clung to the comforting belief that his sin was not his own doing. But Monica's forgiving but pointed messages soon began to arrive, stirring his conscience anew. The longer he stayed in Rome, the more restless he grew. He made excuses for avoiding Bemas and other Manichaean ceremonies. *I will remain a member for now*, thought Augustine. *But forever? Who knows?*

"Alypius! The most amazing thing has transpired!"

"What is it, Augustine? *What?*" Alypius had not seen his friend this animated for a long time.

"Symmachus, the city prefect, has been commanded to select a rhetoric professor for the city of Milan!" The emperor and the imperial court now resided in Milan because of the barbarian threat to Rome. Augustine pounded the table in mingled exultation and anxiety.

"Of course, he'll award the position to you," said Alypius.

"Award it to me? I am trying to decide whether I should even apply for it! I do not posses the experience and influence of many in Rome."

"But you are brilliant and widely known after living in Rome for only a year; there is no question you are one of the best speakers and writers in the city," insisted Alypius.

"Some still regard me as a rustic," protested Augustine. "I speak with a North African accent!"

"Which diminishes daily. But your North African ties have already come in quite handy. Since Symmachus served as proconsul in Carthage for a year or two, he knew your work and reputation before you arrived in Rome."

"It is true his recognition of me has opened many doors." Augustine knew a number of excellent scholars with no local connections had found Rome inhospitable.

"You need only make an address before Symmachus and ask Gallio's brother and Brutus to recommend you," insisted Alypius.

Augustine looked at his companion. Alypius had never flattered him, nor lied, even when it was polite to do so. "Perhaps I should at least try."

"Of course you should," said Alypius. "And I will apply

for a transfer so I can accompany you to Milan." He spoke matter-of-factly, as if his own career was of little importance.

Augustine stared at Alypius in wonder. *How can I be blessed with a friend such as this?*

The horses stamped and neighed in the early fall morning chill. Augustine shivered and drew his cloak around him as he peered down the street, looking for Alypius. Adeodatus did likewise.

"They say the cold usually does not arrive this early here in Rome," said Augustine. "But we'd better get used to chilly weather. Milan is close to the Alps, much farther north than we've ever been."

"I want to see lots of snow," said Adeodatus. "So does Mother." Augustine's concubine would travel with a later caravan, bringing their servants and household goods.

"You'll no doubt see plenty," said Augustine. Ordinarily, icy weather dismayed him; he thoroughly disliked the raw winters of Thagaste during his boyhood. But this morning the brisk air only brought a smile to his face. *Even if Milan's winters are worse than those in the mountains of Numidia, it will be worth it.*

Augustine spotted Alypius as he rode, grinning, up to greet them.

"This still seems a dream," said Augustine.

"I never doubted it for a moment," said Alypius, dismounting. "Not only were you the only intelligent choice for professor of rhetoric because of your ability, but politically it made so much sense. Symmachus is a pagan; he certainly did not want to send a dyed-in-the-wool Catholic Christian to help Ambrose, the bishop, gain more power, especially after he opposed him in past matters. Although Symmachus, like many Roman aristocrats, tries to preserve the ancient religion, he dared not appoint a pagan like himself. It was important the person who holds this position have Christian connections. A Manichaean Christian suits his purposes well. To Symmachus, a Manichaean seems almost a pagan."

"Perhaps he is right," said Augustine. His mind stirred uneasily. He had grown increasingly disillusioned with Manichaeanism, yet his Manichaean references, he felt sure, had helped tip the scales in his favor.

"But let us not speak of political maneuvering and other useless foolery," said Alypius, noticing his friend's darkening face. "Today we celebrate the beginning of your fame and fortune, so justly deserved."

"I would never have gained it without your encouragement, Alypius," said Augustine gratefully. "And I can't believe you arranged your own transfer so quickly."

"I just make sure I know the right people," said Alypius, "and that they know me! We'd better join Symmachus's group before they leave us here in Rome. Race you there!"

Augustine and Adeodatus vaulted onto their horses. The adult adventurers careened wildly through the streets of Rome as they had done as youths in Carthage, Adeodatus on their heels. The newly-awakened sounds of the city rushed past their ears. The sun burst over the horizon as they pounded their way toward the caravan that would guide them to a new destiny.

four

Augustine walked along the wide boulevard on his way to the new basilica in Milan. *Perhaps by now Ambrose has finished his afternoon appointments so we can talk.* He knew the famous bishop filled his days with important ecclesiastical meetings, as well as his sacramental duties. Ambrose conferred with many nobles of the court and even the young emperor himself on a regular basis. *Not surprising that he has little time to devote to a foreigner.*

But everyone in Milan seemed a foreigner! Augustine knew differently, but even in Rome he had not seen such diversity in population. He passed the elegant palace of Emperor Valentinian II, protected by squads of barbarian soldiers. Most citizens of Milan hated the Goths, who arrogantly patrolled their streets and smiled impudently at their wives and daughters. But the boy emperor, who was fighting to retain control of his empire, needed their presence. Augustine avoided eye contact with the brawny, sinister guards; they made him realize afresh he now resided close to a frontier largely uncontrolled by Roman civilization.

The wild, magnificent Alps outside the double wall of the city dwarfed him every time he viewed them. Today heavy gray clouds drifted past their massive white peaks.

But I am glad Milan is so accepting of the rest of us! Although he occasionally encountered prejudice and ignorance about his North African background, he felt at home in the royal court sooner than he had expected. A North African official was not at all unusual. Persians, Germanics, Alexandrians—those involved in military and intelligence matters—daily arrived in Milan. Nor were his Manichaean ties considered unique. The imperial court included pagan sympathizers, Goths, and even Arians, who believed God the Father was of a greater and purer divinity than that of the Son. Justina, the emperor's mother, championed Arian doctrines. Augustine shook his head in amazement. Such a stand would surely have provoked persecution or at least censure in many Christian cities. He knew Ambrose, as the Catholic bishop of Milan, waged a courteous but intense war against Justina's influence. For himself, he felt relief his own Manichaean reputation raised few eyebrows, at least so far.

Augustine gestured with his hand; a street food vendor scrambled to serve him. Augustine made a face as he munched; how did they make bread so tough in Milan? If he had had time, he would have gone home to eat!

But the work here has certainly been enjoyable. It is refreshing to make more than enough money than we need and pleasant to be cordially greeted by the wealthy and powerful. Augustine formulated polished speeches that kept various diplomats and bureaucrats informed—but not too informed—of Emperor Valentinian's official policies. He delivered eulogies for members of the court that exalted them far beyond even their own estimation. These speeches established his reputation as an orator in Milan. He taught some of the most gifted people he had ever encountered. *A far cry from those idiots in Carthage who used to barge into my lectures when and if they pleased!*

He luxuriated in the profoundly intellectual atmosphere of Milan. Clergymen and prosperous laymen alike read Greek classics. Poets considered Milan their Mecca.

But Augustine, who had steadily loosened his Manichaean ties, refused to commit himself to any school of thought. He had revived his interest in Cicero, who advised his disciples to weigh intellectual issues with caution, not accepting any one view. Augustine determined he would continue his lifelong quest for wisdom but would carefully examine and question every idea that came his way. *No more starry-eyed schoolboy nonsense. Will I ever find actual truth?* He did not know. His despair had covered his first weeks in Milan with a cold, dull blanket that his success could not warm.

Augustine turned the corner and quickened his steps, as the church and its buildings still lay some distance away. Knowing the influence of Bishop Ambrose, Augustine had called on him during his first week in Milan and found him pleasant, even fatherly. Such a gracious, concerned welcome contrasted with the bored responses of other powerful officials. Augustine had no intention of endearing himself once more to the Manichaeans of the city, yet he missed the instant Manichaean family that had materialized in Carthage and Rome. Ambrose had made him feel at home in Milan.

I will hear him preach this Sunday, Augustine had told himself after the encounter. Even pagans usually attended services to avoid controversy and make positive connections with clergymen and their parishioners. *Besides, the man's reputation has grown continually these past few years. And Mother never ceases to mention him.* Augustine

45

and Monica now communicated frequently. In his loneliness, Augustine had not resisted her suggestion that she come to Milan in the spring. *Maybe to hear Ambrose as much as to see us.* Augustine smiled a little as he remembered her constant veneration of the bishop.

But he is a superb speaker, Augustine had soon realized as he stood with the other parishioners that Sunday, listening as Ambrose spoke from the bishop's throne. *He addresses us as an educated man, in a refined style with references to Plato, Plotinus, and Cicero.* Augustine's lip curled as he analyzed Ambrose's Bible text; he did not realize his Manichaean bias was guiding his thinking. *I have no patience with the ridiculous Old Testament passage which seems to be the center of his sermon. But his rhetorical techniques are flawless.* Augustine could not resist such an oratorical feast. He had appeared at church the following Sunday to hear Ambrose, and then the next.

Gradually the content of Ambrose's sermons had made an impact on Augustine. Later he wrote: "I was drawing nearer, gradually and unconsciously. For, although I took no trouble to learn what he said, but only to hear how he said it. . .yet, along with the eloquence I prized, there also came into my mind the ideas which I ignored; for I could not separate them."[1] Augustine had always scorned the Old Testament, which North African clergymen interpreted in a very literal way. But when Ambrose explained the Old Testament law and prophets in allegories, Augustine's objections, colored by Manichaean thought, evaporated.

But I still don't think I should follow Catholic Christianity, thought Augustine. *I see now that educated people can support its views without compromising their intellectual integrity. But learned men follow Manichaean views, too.*

The dark clouds snuffed out the bleak winter sunshine, and the wind began to blow harder as Augustine arrived at the episcopal palace. *What am I doing here?* he asked himself. *I myself have an endless number of duties to perform, important people to see. I have no appointment with Ambrose. I will find myself waiting in a cold room while others talk with him.* He paused at the door. *I am weary of debating first one point of view, then another, yet I must. Ambrose gives me no peace, yet I am obliged to seek him.*

Augustine stamped his feet in disgust, then entered the palace.

Augustine's mistress rubbed his broad shoulders, then offered him a cup of wine. He growled slightly in acknowledgment and returned to his glum reverie. She sighed. Augustine had been so taciturn lately! His interest in the sermons of the bishop Ambrose gratified her, as she herself was Catholic. But he became so moody after his occasional short meetings with the famous clergyman. After Ambrose's Sunday sermon, every Monday began with a cloud over Augustine and the entire household. Adeodatus, now an adolescent, could sometimes cajole him out of his dark state. She rejoiced when Nebridius had joined his friends in Milan. When Alypius and Nebridius prodded Augustine into a debate, she caught a glimpse of the fiery, joyous spirit that had drawn her to him years ago in Carthage. He rarely fought with her now, and she missed it. When she spoke to him, he did not hear.

Augustine had received letters, she knew, from North Africa since they had moved to Milan. She herself could not read or write, and he would not answer her questions about their content. She had prayed fervently about them, but her purposeless prayers seemed to drift into nothing.

Would the holy God listen to the prayers of a concubine, anyway? She did not know.

"He was reading silently," said Augustine. His voice cracked the silence with the suddenness of a broken dish.

"Who? Who was reading?"

"Ambrose," said Augustine, as if they had been conversing all along. "Alypius and I wandered into his study, and he was reading."

"Without speaking?" The woman had never heard of such a thing, as all who read or studied in the Roman Empire did so aloud.

"Without saying a word. Perhaps he is trying not to strain his voice; he speaks daily in the mass, you know. And he talks constantly with endless numbers of people. Anyway, he sat there and devoured his book as if it were honey."

"What did you do?" She wanted to keep this conversation going as long as she could, even though it meant little to her.

"Alypius and I just sat and watched him, and after a time we left so that he could study. Such intense contemplation!"

"Why ever would he say nothing of what he was learning?"

"Perhaps if Ambrose read aloud something especially interesting, others would want to discuss it with him. Sometimes even Ambrose needs time to think and pray in quiet."

"Indeed, we all do," said a familiar voice from the door. "Even Ambrose."

Augustine jumped up and ran to Monica, whom he had not seen in more than a year and a half. He threw his arms around her like a boy. Adeodatus, laughing until his voice broke, as it often did these days, dropped her baggage and danced clumsily around them. "I found Grandmother out-side, but we kept the secret! We kept the surprise!"

In the midst of the celebration, no one noticed Adeodatus's mother. She slipped from the room, her face expressionless, her fist to her mouth.

"How was your journey, Mother?" Augustine asked. "It has been a reluctant spring here, with many storms."

Monica smiled. "Traveling was not easy," she admitted. "At one point, the sailors despaired of our safety. I had to encourage them, as God had sent me a dream that reassured me of our safe arrival in Italy."

Augustine laughed. Some things did not change. "He has told me I will live to see you baptized as a Christian," said Monica. "I have no fear he will change His word."

Augustine shook his head in amused frustration, but he said, "Mother, I am no longer a Manichaean. I have decided to become a catechumen in the church." As a catechumen, Augustine was professing a preliminary faith in Christ and a willingness to receive instruction in the teachings of the church. This did not necessarily mean he would soon be get-ting baptized. Like Augustine's father, many catechumens avoided baptism until they were elderly because, for most people at that time, it involved celibacy even if they were married. But to Augustine's mother, becoming a catechumen was a significant step.

To Augustine's surprise, Monica did not show amaze-ment or much emotion at all. She had wept and prayed many hours to hear such a declaration from her son but now received the news calmly. "To what do we owe this change, Augustine?"

"It is advantageous to be known as a Catholic Christian in Milan," he said carelessly. "Far more than to be known

as a Manichaean. And the sermons of Ambrose are interesting. I find him well-educated and provocative."

Monica nodded agreeably, then related news from
Thagaste. But hours later she lay awake, too saturated with
joy to sleep, despite her exhaustion. *Oh, Lord, You are
faithful. You will keep Your promises. I will wait and watch
You work.*

Monica, of course, did not remain idle while she watched
God work. "To thee, O Fountain of mercy, she poured out
still more frequent prayers and tears that thou wouldst has-
ten thy aid and enlighten my darkness."[2] She adroitly
rearranged Augustine's household. She also spent many
hours exploring Milan with Adeodatus. She attended mass
every day, rejoicing in the opportunity to hear her beloved
Ambrose preach. "She loved that man as an angel of God,
since she knew that it was by him that I had been brought
thus far to that wavering state of agitation I was now in,
through which she was fully persuaded I should pass from
sickness to health," wrote her son years later.[3] Ambrose
himself commented on her fervent Christian piety, still not
realizing her son did not fully share her zeal.

As was customary in North Africa, Monica baked special saints' cakes and breads, and loaded them into a basket with choice wine to pass at martyrs' shrines, where she
assumed worshipers would eat together, as they had in
Thagaste.

"You shall not enter with that food," said the shrine's
doorkeeper sternly.

Monica, who normally would have withered the man
with a single glance, stopped short. "I am not allowed to
worship at the grave of the blessed saint?"

"Bishop Ambrose has forbidden feasting at shrines."

"Then I must obey," she murmured and returned home to question Augustine.

"Ambrose believes such practices emulate those of the heathen, who do so to strengthen the spirits of their dead ancestors," said Augustine. "And many people visit multiple shrines, becoming drunk and engorging themselves like so many pigs. Ambrose views this as sacrilegious and will not allow even the temperate sharing of food and drink because of the spiritual danger to the intemperate."

Monica nodded. "I have seen too many who cannot rise from one grave to visit another because of their gluttony and drunkenness," she said and took her basket to share with the poor.

Augustine could not believe his ears! At Ambrose's word, his mother had abandoned the practice of a lifetime without a word of protest.

"I should have asked her for some of those saints' cakes," he told Alypius and Nebridius later. "Who knows when she will bake them again?"

But Monica had other important things to do. Augustine was now thirty-two years old. He had achieved a career of high social and political status; sure opportunities for advancement within the imperial government awaited him. While his income was adequate, a distinguished professor of rhetoric needed a lifestyle that reflected that of the rich aristocrats who patronized him. Augustine needed a proper, wealthy wife.

Monica particularly wanted to arrange a firm marriage contract because Augustine's engagement to a Catholic Christian girl might encourage his acceptance of baptism. She used every connection she and her son possessed to arrange a match.

"Augustine, good news!" she rejoiced one day when

51

her son came home for dinner. "Wonderful news, my son!"

"What good news, Mother?" He smiled to see her excitement but felt a slow sinking in his stomach.

"The family of Gaius Publius has consented to your marriage with their daughter! Tertia is healthy and has had every advantage. I do not have to inform you of their wealth and position; everyone in Milan knows the family. They are, of course, Catholic, and attend Ambrose's basilica. With such a match, you can retire to a country estate to study, write, and teach as you wish! You will speak only when you desire to do so."

"That would be wonderful," said Augustine, a little slowly.

"Tertia is also quite lovely," said Monica shrewdly. "Her beautiful older sisters have produced many healthy children. Adeodatus will have brothers and sisters!"

Augustine remembered the brief glimpse he once had caught of the winsome young girl. "But she is a mere child," he said.

"She is ten years old; in two she will be of legal marriageable age," answered his mother.

Silence.

"You must send the concubine away," said Monica.

"That is part of the contract, I assume," said Augustine, not looking at her.

"Yes."

Silence. Then, "It will be done."

Monica left the room, elated and vastly relieved.

The woman who had been Augustine's mistress watched the gray waves break on the ocean shore at the Italian port city of Ostia. Two years before she and Adeodatus had laughed and celebrated their first sight of Italy; Augustine had dragged his weary, seasick body from his cabin to join them. Together they had excitedly disembarked from the ship to welcome adventures in a new country.

Now she stood alone, the cold salt spray stinging her face.

Not completely alone, of course. Augustine had rarely spoken to her after Monica informed her of his approaching marriage and her own imminent departure. But he had insisted on sending the little maid with her to North Africa. A pleasant, prattling girl, and efficient, too. He had also sent generous gifts. They would please her parents.

He could have sent Adeodatus and me from his house with only the clothes on our backs, she thought. Tears spurted from her eyes, surprising her. They poured down her cheeks like the baptismal fonts at the basilica. She had not cried, even when Adeodatus had clung to her and wept. She had soothed him, knowing he would have no future with her. His brilliant mind, so like his father's, belonged in Milan with the learned and the powerful. She was thankful Augustine had not treated Adeodatus as an illegitimate son but had wanted to keep him in his household.

Augustine had avoided her before the departure; it was just as well. Although they had been faithful to each other for fourteen years, she had never been certain that he truly cared for her.

She hailed an old sailor bobbing in a small boat and offered a price. He rolled his eyes but nodded reluctantly. She threw him a tiny bag of coins, then snapped at her maid, who was tossing pebbles into the water. The two entered the boat; the older man paid no attention to her tears, but the younger one looked as if he would like to comfort her. She ignored them both and covered her face anew with her veil as they rowed out to the ship with its impatient, billowing sails.

53

She had already decided to live a celibate life when she returned home. Although she still turned heads in the marketplace, she was not interested in men. Such a decision meant she could once more be admitted to the Eucharist. She could no longer laugh with Adeodatus, or chide him for his clumsiness, or watch his round, boyish face harden into that of a strong young man, but she could pray for him.

Perhaps if I am restored to the Eucharist, she thought, *the holy God will now hear my prayers. . . .*

Augustine spent many hours with Adeodatus, partly because he sought to calm his distraught son, partly because he saw in Adeodatus the wide, dark eyes and full lips of the boy's mother. He buried himself in his books but could not concentrate even on those he loved best. Loneliness tore at him like the beasts at the games. Frustrated at a two-year wait before his marriage, he took another concubine with whom he formed the loosest of attachments. He did not speak of Adeodatus's mother, not even to Alypius and Nebridius, as well-bred gentlemen never mentioned their mistresses. He did not mention her in his early writings.

But fifteen years later, as a bishop, Augustine bared his soul in his writing: "My mistress was torn from my side as an impediment to my marriage, and my heart which clung to her was torn and wounded till it bled."[4]

five

"Sir, please come quickly! Your mother may be in danger!"

Augustine's servant Rufus never interrupted his master's hours of contemplation and study. "Where is she? What's wrong, Rufus?"

"She must be at the basilica, Sir! I have heard that Bishop Ambrose has defied the emperor and refuses to leave it! Your mother went to mass this morning and has not returned!"

Augustine raced into the street toward the church, his mind numb, incredulous. He knew Ambrose had encouraged his parishioners to fill the sanctuary at all hours during Holy Week. *But why is the emperor attacking the church?* He stopped short of the building itself, glimpsing the hated Gothic soldiers surrounding the basilica. Pulling his cloak over his head, Augustine slipped into a dark side street, where an older, well-dressed man had also taken refuge.

"Have you heard what happened?" Augustine asked him.

"Evidently the emperor's mother has demanded this basilica for Arian liturgy," answered the man. "The bishop refused, saying he will not allow such unchristian goings-on, and Emperor Valentinian has sent his loathsome troops to take it by force. My wife goes faithfully each morning to mass; how I wish she had stayed home this morning!"

"My mother also came to church," said Augustine, a lump in his throat.

"They have done no violence yet," answered his companion. "Let us draw closer to the basilica; perhaps we will learn more."

The two men edged toward the lines of soldiers and waited for hours. Hundreds of Milanese citizens glared at the troops, hatred smoldering in their eyes. A few tossed rocks and spat at the Goths. Others heckled or swore at them. The sullen fever of their contempt made Augustine break into a sweat. *How long will both sides restrain themselves? How long before the blood of clergymen, worshipers, and soldiers intermingles on the streets—and within the church itself?*

"Disperse! Disperse!" A court messenger rode up close to the soldiers and faced the crowd on his prancing horse. "By order of the emperor, all are to leave immediately. He has placed a curfew on all courtiers this very night." He halted and looked hard at Augustine. "Disperse, in the name of the emperor!"

There is nothing I can do, Augustine realized. *Nothing at all*. The Goths formed an impenetrable, evil barricade. Sneaking through the guards, bribing them, assaulting them—all seemed equally implausible. Augustine knew the emperor invested large sums of money to train them well and paid them excellent wages. To attempt to get around the guards would be suicide. *My very presence here may mean my demise or at least imprisonment, if Queen Justina has her way.*

His companion turned, locking eyes with Augustine.

He, too, realizes our helplessness. The men stole back through the streets like thieves. "Go with God," said the other. Augustine returned the good-bye, realizing suddenly that he had never asked for the man's name.

Augustine numbly went about his work the next day. *We're all puppets,* he mused bitterly as he watched other courtiers smile, greet, and perform their usual duties. He knew very well their business-as-usual demeanor covered tense, fearful hearts like his. *But we dare not say anything. Who knows what Valentinian will do, a fifteen-year-old king who one day pleases himself, and the next wishes to please his mother, an Arian!* Augustine knew Ambrose would never give up his church to a ruler who insisted the divinity of God the Father far superceded that of Jesus Christ. He could only pray the emperor's more sensible counselors would intervene. According to reports Augustine had heard, the bishop had shouted to the soldiers that he would rather be executed than leave the basilica.

But I cannot face the loss of my mother, Augustine told himself miserably. *I have lost my love, and I cannot lose my mother, too. It is unthinkable that Gothic bullies would ravage or kill her. Oh, God. Oh, God. . . .* He prayed fervently all day.

That night as he picked at his food and tried to reassure a terrified Adeodatus, a familiar voice stunned them both: "Is *that* a meal for my grandson?" Augustine clasped Monica fervently; Adeodatus held onto her as if he would never let go.

"God has rescued me once more," she assured them, smiling. But her ordeal had drained her face of color, and her thin hands trembled. "God told me I would live to see you baptized, Augustine, and I know He keeps His promises."

"How did you escape?" asked her son, his face as white as hers. "Did anyone follow you?" He rushed to the window.

"Have no fear," answered Monica. "God gave us peace while we were imprisoned in the basilica. Ambrose led us in singing the praises of God as the soldiers threatened us. I have never heard such wonderful melodies! But He also granted our bishop grace in the sight of the emperor; Valentinian listened and repented of his actions. The soldiers had to allow all of us—including Ambrose—to leave the church. You should have seen his face, shining like an angel's! The young emperor will think twice before he does such a foolish thing again. You need not worry, Augustine." She looked at their supper with distaste. "This is not a meal. Where is that worthless servant who would serve you such garbage?"

"Have mercy, Mother. The entire household has been upset," said Augustine. He had almost collapsed from relief. Now he felt too weary to endure her making a scene. "I will have her bring us something else."

For the first time Monica wilted and pressed her fingers to her temples. She admitted, "I am spent. We had nothing to eat except the Host for almost two days."

The basilica incident drew Augustine's attention to Ambrose more than ever. What kind of man refused to bow to one of the most powerful monarchs on earth?

Ambrose, unlike Augustine, was born into a family of wealth and position. He excelled in his classical education, then followed a distinguished legal career until he secured the governorship of Liguria, the province that included the city of Milan. But the Catholic community one day acclaimed him as bishop, even though he was still a catechumen and had not yet been baptized. Despite Ambrose's attempts to decline the demands of the people, the emperor had confirmed the appointment, and Ambrose had then accepted it as God's will.

Now, instead of using every source at his disposal to escape the bishopric, Ambrose reversed his actions: He was baptized by Simplicianus, a senior priest. He gave away his wealth to the poor, then plunged into the formidable task of learning theology as he ministered and taught. He became a famous theologian and speaker, but he also possessed a pragmatic side. Despite severe criticism from fellow clergymen, he melted down some of the gold from the walls of his churches to relieve the poverty of famine-struck, suffering Christians.

Ambrose, a man of enormous charisma and political instinct as well as faith and learning, became the spiritual counselor of several emperors. He chose to be their servant by using his considerable political power to uphold and preserve their sovereignty. But at great risk to himself, he did not hesitate to rebuke or discipline them when they practiced poor judgment. The boy emperor Valentinian II had given in to his advisors' demands to release Ambrose from the basilica only because he recognized the awesome power exerted by the bishop over his subjects. His own counselors would chain him to prison walls if Ambrose commanded it, said Valentinian sulkily.

Because the famous bishop influenced important politicians, church officials, and aristocrats, as well as his parishioners, Augustine could not secure many private appointments with him. And although the bishop wrote prolifically, Augustine did not often pursue his literary works. He preferred to listen every Sunday to the diminutive, slender man with the enormous dark eyes and long, sensitive face, who fascinated him with his learned sermons that wove the ideas of pagans together with those of the Scriptures.

"What, therefore, is more absurd than to link the eternity of the work of creation with the eternity of God the omnipotent?" asked Ambrose. "Or to identify the creation itself with God so as to confer divine honors on the sky, the earth, and the sea? From this opinion there proceeds the belief that parts of the world are gods."[1]

Augustine strained to hear every word.

"Pythagoras maintains that there is one world. Others say that the number of worlds is countless, as was stated by Democritus, whose treatment of the natural sciences has been granted the highest authority by the ancients. That the world always was and always will be is the claim of Aristotle. On the other hand, Plato ventures to assert that the world did not always exist, but that it will always exist. . . . How is it possible to arrive at an estimate of the truth amid such warring opinions?[2]

"Under the inspiration of the Holy Spirit, Moses, a holy man, foresaw that these errors would appear among men and perhaps had already appeared. At the opening of his work he speaks thus: 'In the beginning God created heaven and earth.' He linked together the beginnings of things, the Creator of the world, and the creation of matter in order that you might understand that God existed before the beginning of the world or that He was Himself the beginning of all things."[3]

Hypnotized by Ambrose's wide spectrum of philosophical knowledge, Augustine did not realize the Sunday morning sermon lasted three hours.

When Ambrose speaks of the nature of God, I understand it, marveled Augustine. But the bishop's blunt declaration of personal responsibility for sin made Augustine squirm: "If evil has no beginning, as if uncreated or not made by God, from what source did nature derive it? Because no rational being has denied that evil exists in a world like this in which accident and death are so frequent. Yet from what we have already said we can gather that evil is not a living substance, but is a deviation of mind and soul away from the path of true virtue, a deviation which frequently steals upon the souls of the unaware. The greater danger is not, therefore, from what is external to us, but from our own selves. Our adversary is within us, within us is the author of error, locked, I say, within our very selves. Look closely on your intentions; explore the disposition of your mind; set up guards to watch over the thoughts of your mind and the cupidities of your heart. You yourself are the cause of your wickedness; you yourself are the leader of your own crimes and the instigator of your own misdeeds. Why do you summon an alien nature to furnish an excuse for your sins?"[4]

Sometimes I wish I were still a Manichaean, Augustine thought. *It was so convenient to blame something besides myself for my sins.* His sexual desires tormented him day and night.

My search for answers has wearied me to the point of exhaustion; I am so tired of questioning everything.

Later Augustine would look back to that difficult period of his life: "O crooked ways! Woe to the audacious soul which hoped that by forsaking thee it would find some better thing! It tossed and turned, upon back and side and belly—but the bed is hard, and thou alone givest it rest."[5]

Augustine often debated Ambrose's latest sermon with Romanianus, his old patron who had traveled to Italy in an attempt to settle a longstanding lawsuit that still plagued him. Alypius and Nebridius joined them, and the former Manichaean devotees labored to understand the bishop's revolutionary ideas.

"How is Father today?" Adeodatus asked his grandmother.

"Fine," answered Monica absently. She surveyed her pantry and mentally listed her purchases. But then she turned back to her grandson. "Why do you ask?"

Adeodatus squirmed a little under her measured gaze. "He's been so irritable lately. I thought maybe Father might be sick, or maybe he's been working too hard."

"He seems much better today; he spent yesterday discussing our bishop's last sermon with Alypius, Nebridius, and Romanianus. He always appears refreshed and relaxed after their sessions." His grandmother crossed her arms. "But why the special concern?"

Adeodatus dropped his gaze. "I need some money," he muttered.

"And you wanted to insure his good mood before you asked? Diplomatic, but not necessarily effective," said Monica. "If the money is for books, perhaps you will succeed. If it is for the theater, circus, or baubles for a girl—"

"It is for a book," said Adeodatus. He glared at his grandmother.

Monica smiled and handed him a few coins from a jar in her pantry. "It is good you love books, as he does."

Adeodatus planted a loud, hasty kiss on her cheek and thundered out the door. His grandmother shook her head, smiling. He was so like Augustine at that age. Impulsive, passionate, yet intellectual, with a mind that never stopped questioning his world.

The night before, Augustine himself had returned with an armful of books he had borrowed from his friend Manlius Theodorus. "Look, Mother," he had said eagerly, "here are some treatises by Plotinus! Although I hated Greek and never learned it well, I've always wanted to study Greek classics. Some have been translated into Latin, but I've never found any based on Plato's teaching! But Marius Victorinus, a North African, translated these. "

"It's quite late, and you haven't felt well," said Monica. "Surely you're not going to start reading now?" She knew Augustine always lost track of time when he read. He might even stay up all night. Then he would grow even grouchier.

"I'm just going to look them over," he answered and escaped to his rooms.

Augustine devoured Plotinus's philosophy. His oil lamp often burned into the wee hours as he examined the books. Beauty, Plotinus argued, had to be based on something besides his own opinion, or that of others, and existed far beyond what the senses perceived. It did not consist solely of pleasing symmetry and pattern. True beauty emanated from the Good and was reflected in the soul and intellect of man. "It is, therefore, rightly said, that the beauty and good of the soul consists in her similitude to the Deity; for from hence flows all her beauty."[6]

Plotinus's ideas about beauty intrigued Augustine, as they ran so contrary to what he and others had written about the subject. This Good or Deity, Plotinus believed, did not lie passively, allowing a separate evil force to usurp it, as in Manichaean thought. Instead, the Good aggressively poured itself into everything else in the universe, yet was separate from it. Evil rebelled against the Good, which was a far larger and more potent presence. "But evil is never permitted to remain by itself alone, on account of the superior power and nature of good."[7]

Day and night Augustine pondered the ideas he was reading. Plotinus urged him to examine his own intellect and soul in order to discover God. *Help me, O Lord,* prayed Augustine. *Open the eyes of my soul. If You and Your wisdom truly exist, help me to find You.* He relentlessly probed his heart and mind and saw what he later described as an unchangeable Light.

"It was higher, because it made me, and I was below it, because I was made by it. He who knows the Truth knows that Light. . . . Love knows it, O Eternal Truth and True Love and Beloved Eternity! Thou art my God to whom I sigh both night and day. When I first knew thee, thou didst lift me up, that I might see that there was something to be seen, though I was not yet fit to see it. . . . I trembled with love and fear. I realized that I was far away from thee in the land of unlikeness, as if I heard thy voice from on high: 'I am the food of strong men; grow and you shall feed on me; nor shall you change me, like the food of your flesh into yourself, but you shall be changed into my likeness.' "[8]

Monica had no idea Christ drew her son near through his reading Neoplatonic philosophy. But she poured out fervent prayers for Augustine every waking hour. "God, You have promised I will see my son baptized before I die. I know You keep Your promises." Her tears rained on the bread she was kneading. "Please, let it be soon. Please."

six

"How I *hate* this," Augustine muttered, as he forced himself to begin a panegyric for the emperor, a speech full of official—and mostly false—praise for the less-than-beloved monarch. Augustine gritted his teeth.

I am paid well to think of original, creative ways to lie. I know they are lies. The courtiers who listen know they are lies. Even the emperor, egotistical as he is, knows they are lies. Yet I must perform this travesty and receive a hundred compliments for my expertise.

"Sir, Alypius and Manlius Theodorus to see you." His servant hovered uncertainly outside the door.

"By all means, send them in!" *I'll do this later tonight. Perhaps my friends can inspire me!*

Alypius grinned as he entered. "Sure we are not interrupting you?"

"You know perfectly well nothing could delight me more. But don't flatter yourself. I am writing a loathsome panegyric and would welcome a barbarian with a head ax. Greetings, Manlius."

The tall, distinguished man bowed. "I, too, weary of studying and writing. Let's go to the theater and rest our brains."

Augustine rarely attended the theater, even though he had loved it to the point of obsession as a teenager in Carthage. Manlius noticed his hesitation. "Such drivel does not nourish the mind," he admitted. "But no one should remain serious at all times. Come with us, Augustine. I have a sumptuous supper prepared for us afterward, and then we can soothe our consciences by having a deep, dark discussion."

"Nebridius, Zenobius, and Hermogenianus will join us, as well as Romanianus. You must come!" said Alypius.

Augustine threw down his pen. "I give up!" The two hurried him out the door before he could change his mind.

"Was it not worth it?" asked Alypius as they made their way home through the darkened streets.

"It certainly was." *My friends chose well,* thought Augustine. He had found the play both entertaining and thought-provoking. Manlius frequently hosted the circle of friends at his beautiful villa. Wealthy and highly educated, he had retired from public life and now spent his hours writing books on philosophy. *He keeps the best cook in Milan,* thought Augustine, *and the best wine. But the discussion satisfied me even more than those.*

Yet anxiety already had eroded Augustine's euphoria. He really must complete the panegyric tonight so he could polish it tomorrow and practice it thoroughly before the emperor's celebration. He trudged gloomily through the night, his feet dragging more and more.

A happy song interrupted his dismal reverie. A beggar, clutching a few coins, laughed and joked as he staggered through the streets.

"Lovely, lovely lady," he warbled at the top of his lungs. "Lovely, lovely one. . . ."

"Had a good night down by the theater, perhaps," said Alypius. "He's certainly celebrating!"

"I wouldn't mind trading places with him right now," said Augustine heavily.

"You'll feel better after you finish the panegyric," sympathized Alypius. "I, too, must deal with idiots who possess the morality of jackals. But would we truly prefer the life of a beggar?"

"Of course not. Yet such a possibility still tempts me—me, with my distinguished profession, my superior education, my abundant income. Above all, I wish to be happy. But this beggar is happier than I am!"

The two friends shook their heads and continued on their way.

Augustine later recorded the irony of the encounter in his *Confessions*: "Let my soul take its leave of those who say: 'It makes a difference as to the object from which a man derives his joy. The beggar rejoiced in drunkenness; you longed to rejoice in glory.' What glory, O Lord? The kind that is not in thee, for, just as his was no true joy, so was mine no true glory; but it turned my head all the more. He would get over his drunkenness that same night, but I had slept with mine many a night and risen again with it, and was to sleep again and rise again with it, I know not how many times."[1]

"It seems like an impossible dream!" exclaimed Augustine. "To live together in the country, to free ourselves from maddening distractions of life, to immerse ourselves in the search for wisdom and truth! Such a life staggers the imagination!"

"It is not impossible," said Romanianus. "I must remain here until this interminable lawsuit ends; I can think of no greater pleasure than spending the time with my dearest friends, pursuing the delights of philosophy."

"But few of us can hope to finance such a venture!" objected Augustine. "Nebridius, of course, is quite wealthy. Manlius, too. But the rest of us would struggle. The income from my father's estate is quite meager; I have barely begun to attain any degree of prosperity in my career."

Romanianus smiled. "We can pool our resources," he answered. "And, too, I welcome the opportunity to help make this a reality. I have long dreamed of this, Augustine. Do not deny me the joy of it."

"But you already made my schooling possible," objected Augustine.

"A most profitable investment," answered Romanianus. "If only all my projects turned out this well!"

"I will make this one your best endeavor ever," said Augustine.

Augustine and nine eager friends gathered to discuss their idea. But their utopia did not materialize. Most wanted to leave their professional ambitions behind to retire to a life of study, contemplation, and discussion. But like many secular and religious perfectionists of their era, they envisioned this perfect life of philosophy as totally divorced from the world's concerns, including marriage and family ties.

"I will not leave my wife," said Zenobius flatly, "even to join such a distinguished and amiable company. Nor do I wish my children to grow up without a father's guidance."

"Neither do I," admitted Hermogenianus.

"I am betrothed," said another. "My wedding approaches, and I cannot break my agreement."

Augustine said nothing, but he stared miserably at the floor. He did not want to give up his current concubine, even though their brief and shallow encounters left much to be desired. Since Adeodatus's mother had returned to Africa, he had suffered endlessly from the lack of a stable relationship with a woman. Nor did Augustine wish to renounce his betrothal. *Even though I love my friends and the pursuit of philosophy, I cannot picture an endless lifetime of aching hunger. . . .*

The conversation floundered, and the project with it. But the close friends continued to meet and pursue true wisdom together.

Augustine began to devour the writings of Saint Paul. The Scriptures that had seemed contradictory years before made wonderful sense to him now. "I saw that those pure words had but one face. . . . I found that whatever truth I had read [in the Platonists] was here combined with the exaltation of thy grace."[2]

He discovered amazing kinship in the apostle's struggles: "I find then a law, that, when I would do good, evil is present with me. For I delight in the law of God after the inward man: But I see another law in my members, warring against the law of my mind, and bringing me into captivity to the law of sin which is in my members. O wretched man that I am! Who shall deliver me from the body of this death?" (Romans 7:21–24).

"These thoughts sank wondrously into my heart, when I read that 'least of thy apostles,' and when I had considered all thy works and trembled," wrote Augustine in his *Confessions.*[3]

"I must go see Simplicianus," Augustine told his mother one morning, leaving her to stare after him in surprise and delight. Simplicianus had baptized Ambrose and remained the bishop's close friend and mentor. *He is a wise, well-educated man, and a Christian of many years. Perhaps he can help me.*

The elderly priest welcomed Augustine, noting the dark circles under the young man's eyes and his haggard look. "How have you been, my friend? What occupies your mind these days?"

To Augustine's consternation, tears welled up in his eyes. He steadied his voice and said abruptly, "I am seeking for true wisdom, for the philosophy that leads to truth."

"A worthy quest, Augustine. Admirable. Few men care to make such an important quest. They often simply wish to feel important in their 'pursuit of knowledge.' Where have you wandered in your journey to find truth?"

Augustine told Simplicianus of his venture into Manichaeanism, his decision to renounce any school of thought or religion, his return to Cicero's writings, his fascination with Neoplatonism. "I have been reading Plotinus and Porphyry, as translated by Marius Victorinus."

"Excellent, excellent," murmured the priest. "Unfortunately, many seekers do not encounter philosophical writings that point them to knowing God. In reading the Neoplatonists, one can hardly prevent thoughts of Him. His Word steals in, not to take, but to give."

Simplicianus rose stiffly from his stool and stepped slowly to the window and back. "I must cater to the demands of my old bones from time to time." He smiled at Augustine. "But you may ignore them! Did you find the translations helpful?"

"Oh, yes," answered Augustine.

"I knew Victorinus before he became a Christian," said Simplicianus. "He held the position of rhetor of Rome, as you do of Milan. An intelligent man, a pagan who reaped the admiration of senators. They even erected a statue of him in the forum."

Victorinus must have been a brilliant scholar to have

merited such an expression of esteem, Augustine knew.

"Victorinus not only knew the classics, but he read the Holy Scriptures as well," said Simplicianus. "After carefully investigating them, he told me privately he believed in Jesus Christ. I replied, 'I shall not believe it, nor shall I count you among the Christians until I see you in the Church of Christ.'

"Victorinus laughed and said: 'Is it then the walls that make Christians?'[4] It became a sort of private joke between us. But God was working in the man's heart. He began to realize he bowed to the prejudices of others against Christianity. He did not want to antagonize his aristocratic pagan friends. But Victorinus dreaded the thought of Christ's denying him before the Father because he himself refused to acknowledge their friendship on earth. One day, with no warning, he said, 'Let us go to the Church; I wish to become a Christian.'[5] I was overcome with joy and accompanied him," said Simplicianus, his eyes shining at the memory. "Despite the opposition he encountered and the loss of prestige and wealth, Victorinus was not ashamed to become like a newborn baby in Christ and to bear the stigma of the cross.

"When you ponder the writings of the Neoplatonists," added Simplicianus, "meditate on the labor of God in the heart of the man who translated them so that you, too, might find the true wisdom."

All through the summer of 386, Augustine struggled. "With increasing anxiety I was going about my usual affairs, and daily sighing to thee. I attended thy church as frequently as my business, under the burden of which I groaned."[6] He began to suffer pains in his chest that made it difficult for him to speak in public. Despite his mother's efforts to fatten him up, he grew thinner. He slept erratically and often rose in the night to ponder his dilemma until dawn.

For Augustine had determined his real struggle. He realized he had already crossed a line from uncertainty to faith in Christ but dreaded commitment to celibacy, the impossible demand he could not separate from his decision: " 'The Way'—the Saviour himself—pleased me well, but as yet I was reluctant to pass through the strait gate.[7] I had now found the goodly pearl; and I ought to have sold all that I had and bought it—yet I hesitated."[8]

Late Roman culture, pagan and Christian alike, demanded complete celibacy from its foremost philosophers and spiritual leaders. The church at that time did not specifically command its clergy to renounce marriage. Saint Paul, Augustine knew, did not forbid marriage in his writings. But most people of his era, high and low, did not view celibacy as optional for a dedicated Christian. The majority postponed baptism until late life, some because they desired to remain promiscuous, and others because they wanted marriage and children. Augustine's good friend Verecundus refused baptism because he was married—even though his wife had already declared her faith in Christ! Verecundus would have felt obliged to abandon her, even though the Scriptures in reality forbade such an action.

"Grant me chastity and continence, but not yet," Augustine had prayed as a young man. "I was afraid lest thou shouldst hear me too soon, and too soon cure me of my disease of lust which I desired to have satisfied rather than extinguished."[9]

Nothing has changed, Augustine mused grimly. *I cannot give up women. I willingly give up my maddening profession, my money, and property. But I cannot give up women. I cannot.*

That August, in the midst of his mental battle, Augustine

and Alypius, who had joined his household, were surprised by a visit from a fellow North African named Ponticianus. Their guest, an elite officer of the imperial court, was a devout baptized Christian. As the new friends conversed, he noticed a copy of Paul's writings on a table nearby. Excited by the discovery of fellow believers, he asked Augustine and Alypius if they had ever heard of Antony, an Egyptian monk.

"We've never heard of him," they answered.

"Such a holy man! I can't believe you aren't familiar with his amazing love for God," said Ponticianus. He told story after story of the monk's piety while Augustine and Alypius sat openmouthed. "Antony converted his friends, and they began to live in communities characterized by their purity and dedication to God. Monasteries similar to those created by Antony and his group now abound everywhere. Your bishop, Ambrose, supports a monastery outside Milan."

Augustine and Alypius looked at each other. They had no idea such a brotherhood existed near their town!

"Two of my own friends renounced their promising futures and their approaching marriages when they heard the story of Antony," Ponticianus marveled. "One said, 'Tell me, I beg you, what goal are we seeking in all these toils of ours? What is it that we desire? What is our motive in public service? Can our hopes in the court rise higher than to be 'friends of the emperor?' But how frail, how beset with peril, is that pride! Through what dangers must we climb to a greater danger? And when shall we succeed? But if I chose to become a friend of God, see, I can become one now.' "[10] His companion instantly agreed with him. And when my colleagues informed their fiancées of their decision, the women, too, declared they would adopt lives of celibacy and piety, as Antony did!" Ponticianus's emotion overwhelmed him, and he was silent.

After their friend left, Augustine cried to Alypius, "What is the matter with us? What is this? What did you hear? The uninstructed start up and take heaven, and we—with all our learning but so little heart—see where we wallow in flesh and blood!"[11] He stormed out to the garden with Alypius at his heels.

I don't resent your presence, dear friend, Augustine's eyes told Alypius. *I know you care about my suffering.* Augustine gripped his knees. He pulled at his hair, then crushed his chin against his chest in agony.

"It was, in fact, my old mistresses, trifles of trifles and vanities of vanities, who still enthralled me. They tugged at my fleshly garments and softly whispered: 'Are you going to part with us? And from that moment will we never be with you any more?'. . .I hesitated to break loose and shake myself free of them and leap over to the place to which I was being called—for unruly habit kept saying to me, 'Do you think you can live without them?' "[12]

Augustine's battle bowed him to the ground. *I cannot. I cannot.*

A vision of a woman rose before his fevered eyes. She beckoned to Augustine, then opened her hands. People of all ages appeared, cheerful, serene in their celibacy. "And she smiled on me with a challenging smile as if to say: 'Can you not do what these young men and maidens can? Or can any of them do it of themselves, and not rather in the Lord their God?' "[13]

Augustine's sins and weaknesses overwhelmed him. He tore away from Alypius and threw himself under a fig tree. He wept and wept, tears flowing down his face, his hands, his arms, soaking his rich robe.

"Pick it up, read it; pick it up, read it."

Augustine raised his head in consternation. Was a child

watching his agony? *Is he making sport of me?* Augustine searched the garden. Only Alypius stood quietly at the other end. He knew of no children close to his lodging.

"Pick it up, read it."[14] The young voice somehow held a command.

Augustine struggled to his feet in wonder. Ponticianus had related how the monk Antony had renounced his possessions at the reading of Christ's words: "Go and sell what you have and give it to the poor, and you shall have treasure in heaven; and come and follow me."[15] *I must read the Scriptures*, thought Augustine. *God is calling me to pick them up and read.* He stumbled into the house and opened Paul's epistles: "Not in rioting and drunkenness, not in chambering and wantonness, not in strife and envying, but put on the Lord Jesus Christ, and make no provision for the flesh to fulfill the lusts thereof."[16]

"I wanted to read no further, nor did I need to. For instantly, as the sentence ended, there was infused in my heart something like the light of full certainty and all the gloom of doubt vanished away."[17]

Alypius entered silently, his eyes full of anxiety. Augustine beckoned to him with a trembling smile. Together they read the Scriptures.

"I will follow Jesus Christ," Augustine said simply. "He calls me to a life totally devoted to Him, and I have answered yes.

"I will go with you," responded Alypius.

The two friends would minister together throughout their lifetime as bishops. Over and over they would return to that exquisite, painful moment. Augustine, remembering, wrote: "Go on, O Lord, and act: stir us up and call us back; inflame us and draw us to thee; stir us up and grow sweet to us; let us now love thee, let us run to thee."[18]

seven

W here is this villa of which you speak?" asked Monica a short while after Augustine had dedicated himself to following Christ.

"We will stay at Cassiciacum, near Lake Como, in the foothills, Mother. Verecundus says we will find the view of the Alps and the lake spectacular," said Augustine, grinning. *Although my conversion overwhelmed her with joy, she still questions my decisions, as she always has.*

"Does Verecundus know we have little means of paying him for such a lodging?"

"He has offered it rent-free, and proposes to pay our other expenses as well, Mother. Verecundus would go with us, but he refuses to be baptized because of his marriage." Augustine paused. "I am truly glad that I was converted before I married Tertia," he said in a low voice. "It has saved me endless complications." Immediately after his conversion, Augustine had determined that he would be celibate and had broken his betrothal, citing his continued ill health.

"I, too, believe that God changed your plans," Monica assured him, smiling.

Augustine brightened and went to speak to Romanianus about his son Licentius. Augustine had tutored the boy in the past, and wanted him to accompany the group to Cassiciacum. *I need my friends with me. Likewise, Adeodatus will not be happy without someone his own age. Perhaps if his grandmother fusses over another boy, she will stop hovering around me!*

Monica enjoyed watching Augustine as he walked out the door and down the street. Although his chest ailment still troubled him, Augustine looked so much better these past few weeks. Not for anything would Monica have traded the new spring in her son's step, the note of serenity in his voice. While his illness concerned her deeply, it had provided a convenient reason to cancel his marriage contract, and it permitted him to retire from his work without scandal. *Once he breathes that pure mountain air,* Monica told herself, *he will recover quickly.*

She thanked God every day for her son's miraculous conversion and dedication to Christ. *Of course, I will miss the beautiful, brilliant grandchildren I would have had.* She nodded regretfully. *But I have Adeodatus, and both Perpetua and Navigius have children as well. No woman could wish for more.* To her delight, Navigius, who had remained close to his brother, Augustine, had agreed to join them and participate in this philosophical adventure. *It will be wonderful to stay together in a quiet country retreat, praying and discussing the Scriptures.* Monica had found Milan fascinating but noisy and full of intrigues. She would miss hearing Ambrose speak, of course, but the knowledge that her son had shed his radical Manichaeanism to embrace Christianity would more than compensate for the sacrifice.

Although she worried about their finances, Monica lauded Augustine's decision to retire from his position as rhetor of Milan. The job had drained him and forced him into hypocrisies his forthright nature could not bear.

"God has granted my dearest wish," she told an inquisitive sparrow that perched on her windowsill, "and He will care for us, as He cares for you."

The bird chirped an amen, and Monica, laughing, began preparations for their move.

"So you will leave at the beginning of Vintage Holidays?" asked Romanianus. The Vintage Holidays, or *Feriae Vindemiales,* began in early September, when pupils and teachers alike breathed a sigh of relief. Many professors spent their time in leisurely intellectual pursuits during the holidays.

Augustine's genius had attracted the attention of Romanianus even when the Milanese rhetor had been a schoolboy in Thagaste. As a young professor in Carthage, Augustine had converted his patron to Manichaeanism with his persuasive arguments and razor-sharp wit. Together they had made a sincere, although unsuccessful, attempt to create a community in which they and all their friends could pursue philosophy—true wisdom—with heart, soul, and mind. Now Augustine had succeeded by himself.

"Yes, Romanianus, only ten more days, and I will be free to study, pray, and think. I can hardly wait!"

"Your dream has finally come true," agreed Romanianus.

It was just as well Augustine had accomplished this dream without the financial help of Romanianus, as his lawsuit was not going well. But Augustine had confidentially informed his former patron that he planned to retire permanently from his prestigious career. *Why abandon such a position?* thought Romanianus. *Why not go to the country to rest, and return invigorated and ready to climb the professional ladder? Then he could procure an honorable, easy appointment that would help finance a permanent time of creative leisure, not just a temporary one.*

And why had Augustine broken his betrothal? Romanianus shook his head. He seemed determined to commit career suicide.

"Thank you so much for allowing Licentius to go with us. Adeodatus will enjoy our time at Cassiciacum so much more with his presence."

Romanianus did not object to his son's accompanying Augustine. "The boy will learn more on vacation with you than he would during an entire school year with some other teacher," said Romanianus. But Augustine's emotional conversion, his decision to pursue baptism the following spring—these developments concerned his former patron.

"Will you continue to pursue true wisdom?" asked Romanianus.

Augustine placed his hand on the older man's shoulders and looked into his eyes. "More than ever," he reassured him. Augustine had despaired of finding truth when Manichaeanism failed him. Now he believed Christianity would supply the intellectual answers he craved. "I know God will guide our reasoning primarily through His Word. But I will continue to peruse the works of Plotinus, Porphyry, Cicero, Terence, and others, and teach Licentius and Adeodatus, as well as the others, in this vein. I am taking my entire classical library with me, and Verecundus urges us to make use of his extensive collections."

"Thank heaven," said Romanianus. He could not stomach the thought of his brilliant young relative becoming a mindless monk, spouting platitudes that had no intellectual basis.

"You need not fear I will renounce scholarship," said Augustine, amused at his patron's relief. "I will use whatever is necessary to understand true wisdom."

Augustine's joy and confidence soared as he headed home to pack. *I know God Himself guides my passion for truth.*

"Father, look at this centipede!" said Adeodatus. He and Licentius had found the little creature crawling on his notebook. They marveled at its many legs and rippling movement.

"Kill it quickly!" said Monica, who feared an insect invasion of the villa.

Adeodatus obligingly chopped the centipede into several segments, which continued to wriggle and creep across the notebook.

"Can you dissect the life force of this centipede as well?" asked Augustine. "Is its soul also a material object that can be divided?"

He discussed these questions with the boys, then sent them off to search out any relevant philosophical works in the library. "After lunch, I want you to separate and ponder these questions. Adeodatus, you go down by the lake to think. Licentius, I want you to climb that hill. This evening we will discuss the answers and implications. You should be able to defend your point of view, as Alypius and I will also ponder them this afternoon."

"We're beaten already," said Licentius. Bright, but often undisciplined in his habits, he sometimes disliked Augustine's intensive sessions.

"Probably," said Adeodatus cheerfully. "But one day, we will surprise you!"

Augustine grinned a little uneasily. He still outdistanced

his son's immature mind with little effort, but the boy sometimes exhibited flashes of genius that foretold a dazzling intellectual future. "Is this the day, then, you will defeat the old men?"

"Maybe!" The two boys tore into the house with Monica not far behind exhorting them to wipe their feet.

Alypius laughed. "You seem to have found a way to motivate Licentius."

"For today. Keeping that boy on track challenges me more than mastering Aristotle's *Ten Categories*. I hope sending him to the hills this afternoon will not distract him too much. But if he has to climb first, perhaps he will tire himself enough to sit and meditate."

"You are an excellent teacher, Augustine."

Alypius tended to criticize more readily than flatter. Augustine felt a warm glow in the face of such a compliment. "I am convinced that freeing these young minds to seek truth is a far more effective method than all those beatings I took in Thagaste," he answered, then sighed. "I am weary, though. This pain in my chest still torments me from time to time."

"You'd better rest now. We will still have plenty of time to put together a treatise that will leave those boys panting in the dust."

Augustine lay down on a blanket, drinking in the crisp, golden beauty of the day. Because he focused so intently on his inner thoughts, he had often overlooked the loveliness of nature. He now listened closely to the muted rhythms of lake water lapping against the shore, reveled in the rich blue of the sky, savored the perfume of the last flowers before frost. The white peaks of the majestic Alps pointed to God. Augustine spent hours in passionate prayer each day as he drank in his surroundings. *September in*

Cassiciacum. The closest to heaven I'll ever be while on earth. Thank You, Lord. Thank You.

Augustine missed his cultured friends who had considered forming such a community. *It would have been far easier to have done this with Manlius, Zenobius, and the others,* he postulated, *than it has been with Trygetius, Lastidianus, Rusticus, Navigius, and the boys.* Augustine had to repeat basic concepts for Trygetius, a young nobleman. And Augustine's brother often puzzled over Augustine's methods; he struggled with abstract thought, whereas Augustine thrived on it. *Thanks be to God for Alypius!* Their friendship grew daily, it seemed.

The scent of Monica's fragrant breads permeated the morning air each day, as did her prayers for the little group. Augustine knew their days in Cassiciacum would have been far less pleasant and far less profitable without his mother's presence. While possessing little formal education, she nevertheless possessed spiritual insights that sometimes dwarfed Augustine's. She took part in their discussions freely.

Even though Augustine's health limited his activities, he accomplished a great deal during those months. He wrote several treatises, dedicated to his friends back in Milan who soon circulated these new intellectual works in their scholarly circles: *Contra Academicos* (*Against the Skeptics*), which argued against cynics' refusal to adopt a firm intellectual and spiritual stance; *De beata vita (On the Happy Life),* in which true happiness was found through knowing the Triune God; and *De ordine (On Order),* which Augustine wrote in response to a poem by Zenobius. In this treatise, Augustine wrestled with the problem of evil. He asserted that it does not exist as an equal opposite of good, but that Christians can oppose it successfully, as Christ proved. *On*

Order also increased educational boundaries to include the sciences, geometry, and the mathematical basis of astronomy, as well as the traditional history, literature, and rhetoric. But all of these were but preliminary steps to studying religious philosophy, declared Augustine, which was the ultimate method of obtaining truth.

These writings reflect Augustine's confidence in seeking philosophical answers within a Christian framework, an approach as innovative as that of Ambrose, or even more so. But when Augustine wrote his revolutionary *Soliloquia (The Soliloquies)* for his friends, they had never before read such an intimate revelation of an author. He began with a long, personal prayer, then recorded a debate between his own Reason and his Soul, dealing with many issues that perplexed Augustine for years. The two entities argued about Augustine's continued struggle with his sexuality and his reservations in becoming a Christian.

"The more I understand my weakness, the more I comprehend how much I need God," said Augustine to his mother one day as they watched snow fall in the now-blighted garden.

"The longer I know God, the more I recognize how much I must depend on Him to lead a worthy life," said Monica.

"Yet you are baptized," said Augustine.

"Only God's mercy permits us to beg for baptism," said Monica.

"Perhaps it is time that I, too, became a beggar."

Augustine sniffed Milan's warm spring air, heavy with the promise of new life. "Come, Alypius, Adeodatus, let us go to the church. Mother, are you ready? It is time!"

Adeodatus smiled at his father. *Can he really be as tall*

as me? thought Augustine. *How wonderful that he begins his walk of grace at fifteen!* The boy had worn a hair shirt like Augustine's throughout Lent and avoided bathing, as was customary for all *competentes*. Too, Adeodatus had attended Ambrose's extensive prebaptismal instruction faithfully with Augustine. He watched his son drink in every word and prayed Adeodatus would follow Christ with that same passion all his life. *Imagine his wisdom when he reaches my age!*

They walked together to the door of the basilica, where Monica went in to stand with the women in the sanctuary. Augustine's group made its way to the separate baptistery, where the other people about to be baptized gathered in worship. Each baptismal candidate would pass separately through a curtained doorway to the deep pool of water.

For years I avoided baptism as if it were some dread plague. Now I can hardly wait!

As Augustine waited, he thought of a friend from Thagaste, with whom he associated not long after his conversion to Manichaeanism. Augustine had introduced Flavius to his radical new faith, and the two had enjoyed poking fun at the traditionalists around them. They became quite close. Augustine remembered the friendship as "sweeter to me than all the sweetness of my life thus far."[1]

But Flavius contracted a fever and lay critically ill for many days. Augustine helped care for him, staying close to his side. Then he heard his friend's family had had him baptized while he was unconscious. *I thought they were insane! But I figured we'd share a good laugh about it once he was better.* When Flavius had a brief remission of his illness, Augustine had joked with him about his so-called baptism. To his total surprise, the teenager grew livid with anger. Later Augustine would recall the incident: "But he recoiled from me, as if I were his enemy, and with a remarkable and unexpected freedom, he admonished me that, if I desired to continue as his friend, I must cease to say such things."[2] Although distraught, Augustine decided to discuss it with Flavius when he had recovered more fully. But that moment never came.

I left town for only a few days, Augustine thought with regret. *Only a few days. And he died while I was gone. . . . Maddened with grief, I ran off to Carthage, as if that would cure my pain.*

The man in front of Augustine passed through the curtains. Alypius smiled at Augustine. *You're next!* said his eyes.

Augustine rejoiced afresh at the sight of his friend. *I may not have accompanied Flavius in baptism,* Augustine thought, *but Alypius and I will be baptized this day! And some day, old friend,* he told Flavius silently, *we will discuss this matter of baptism together. Only I suspect it will be quite a different conversation from what I had originally planned!*

The doorkeeper beckoned to Augustine, and he entered the baptistery area. He and Ambrose were the only people in the room. Candlelight flickered and gleamed in the water of the large, octagonal pool. A chilly stream gushed from the baptismal fountain. Augustine shed all of his clothing to symbolize his complete renunciation of his old way of life. Then he knelt before Ambrose, who anointed him with oil that flowed freely from his head down to his shoulders and across his back. Augustine rose and turned toward the western wall. He formally renounced Satan and all his works, then turned to the east and affirmed his faith in Jesus Christ.

Ambrose prayed before the baptismal pool and made the sign of the cross. Together they descended into the water.

"Do you believe in God the Father almighty?" asked Ambrose, his dark eyes blazing. Augustine marveled that so small and slender a man could appear so imposing.

"I do believe." Ambrose pressed on Augustine's shoulders, and he felt the frigid bath wash over his face, his eyes, his hair.

"Do you believe in our Lord Jesus Christ and in his cross?"

"I do believe." Augustine dipped below the water's surface once more.

"Do you believe also in the Holy Spirit?"

"I do believe."[3] Augustine was submerged a final time, then ascended from the pool, where Ambrose anointed him once more and gently washed his feet, a gesture which only Milanese churches practiced at that time. Augustine donned a pure white robe and paused at the curtained door that led to the main sanctuary where a large, jubilant congregation would welcome him and his fellow *competentes*. *For the first time I will take Communion. The Holy Spirit of Christ lives within me!*

Augustine closed his eyes and stood in silence, still shivering from the cold water and the enormity of what he had experienced. "The house of my soul is too narrow for thee to come in to me," he prayed. "Let it be enlarged by thee."[4]

He entered the basilica. Monica's face shone from the shadows like an angel's.

eight

S o open your ears and enjoy the good odor of eternal life which has been breathed upon you by the grace of the sacraments," said Ambrose in a homily soon after Augustine's baptism.[1] During the weeks after Easter, the bishop taught his new converts carefully about the Holy Spirit, the sacraments, and the incarnation of Christ.

Augustine could not hear enough. The masses he attended after his baptism stirred his heart and mind as never before: "And so we were baptized, and the anxiety about our past life left us. Nor did I ever have enough in those days of the wondrous sweetness of meditating on the depth of thy counsels concerning the salvation of the human race."[2] Augustine sang the missal hymns with conversion fervor: "How deeply was I moved by the voices of thy sweet-speaking Church! The voices flowed into my ears; and the truth was poured forth into my heart, where the tide of my devotion overflowed, and my tears ran down, and I was happy in all these things."[3]

Augustine, Adeodatus, and Alypius all wore special ceremonial sandals after their baptism which symbolized their new walk in Christ. *I think I could walk straight to heaven in these*, thought Augustine.

"Thou hast anointed my head with oil, and Thy inebriating cup, how excellent it is!" said Ambrose.[4]

But Augustine did not spend his time in mere euphoria. He had already finished his *De immortalitate animae (On the Immortality of the Soul)*. After his baptism, Augustine began to write a set of textbooks on various disciplines: arithmetic, dialectic, geometry, grammar, philosophy, and rhetoric. The last, *De musica (On Music)*, he finished later in Thagaste. Such textbooks, he hoped, would ultimately lead their readers to God, the basis of all wisdom.

Evodius, a former member of the emperor's secret police, eagerly joined Augustine's household in Milan not long after their baptism. Disgusted by the intrigues of his former occupation, Evodius had already renounced the world and chosen baptism. He and Augustine carried on dialogues that eventually resulted in Augustine's works *De animae quantitate (On the Greatness of the Soul)* and *De libero arbitrio (On Free Will)*.

"Alypius," said Augustine one evening as everyone gathered around a cool fountain to relax, "I believe God is changing my desire to remain in Milan, which swells with churches and much learning. Surely we could be more useful elsewhere."

"Such as?"

"Such as Thagaste." Augustine smiled sheepishly.

"I thought you said you never wanted to live in that backward little rat hole again."

"Augustine!" remonstrated Monica. "You called our hometown a rat hole?"

"Years ago, Mother. Every young man thinks his hometown is a rat hole." He frowned at Alypius, who smiled innocently.

"I hardly remember mine," said Adeodatus. "So how can I think Carthage a rat hole?"

"It most certainly is not," said Monica. "At any rate, you are seriously considering a return to Thagaste?"

"Yes," said Augustine. "I am. I pray daily that God will show us His holy will. I believe He has a special purpose in mind for our group."

"We will pray with you," said Alypius, and Evodius nodded. They all joined to sing a portion of Psalm 119 as they watched the stars come out:

> *Teach me, O LORD, the way of thy statutes;*
> *   and I shall keep it unto the end.*
> *Give me understanding, and I shall keep thy law;*
> *   yea, I shall observe it with my whole heart.*
> *Make me to go in the path of thy commandments;*
> *   for therein do I delight.*
> Psalm 119:33–35

"What a strange town Ostia is!" said Monica later that year as they entered the outskirts of the seaport about sixteen miles southwest of Rome. Formerly a bustling, prosperous city, it now struggled economically because of the unrest in the empire that frequently interfered with trade. Gorgeous mansions of Roman aristocrats intermingled with miserable homes in need of repair. Unruly lower class crowds swarmed the harbor area. Yet noble Christian families still retained residences in Ostia. To Augustine's surprise, he and his group had been invited to stay in the opulent summer home of the Anicii family, the richest in Rome. *Probably Ambrose's influence,* thought Augustine. *He is famous throughout the empire.*

Augustine thanked the Anicii for their gracious reception.

Now his mother could lodge luxuriously while they waited for a good, strong wind to carry them to Africa. Their trip from Milan of well over three hundred miles had exhausted her. He himself needed rest.

Augustine loved the little salon they could use for discussions; statues of philosophers lined its walls, and one could view the lovely gardens from the numerous windows.

"Still fragrant although autumn approaches," said Augustine one day as they sat together in the sunshine. He inhaled deeply.

"And so colorful! Sometimes I wonder how flowers will appear in heaven," said Monica.

"I try to imagine the lives of the redeemed of God in heaven," said Augustine.

Monica and Augustine shared a comfortable long silence. Then began a conversation Augustine would remember all his life. The mother and son spoke of Christ, the perfect, heavenly Light. "O Lord, thou knowest that on that day we were talking thus and that this world, with all its joys, seemed cheap to us even as we spoke."[5] Nothing, agreed Monica and Augustine, could begin to compare with the eternal ecstasy of knowing Him. "We gradually passed through all the levels of bodily objects, and even through the heaven itself, where the sun and moon and stars shine on the earth. Indeed, we soared higher yet by an inner musing, speaking and marveling at thy works."[6] When they could finally speak, they agreed "if to any man the tumult of the flesh were silenced. . .if the very soul grew silent to herself, and went beyond herself by not thinking of herself; . . .if then he alone spoke, not through them but by himself, that we might hear his word, not in fleshly tongue or angelic voice, nor sound of thunder, nor the obscurity of a parable, but might hear him. . .we then with rapid thought might touch on that Eternal Wisdom which abides over all."[7]

The glory of the vision ebbed and flowed like the tranquil Mediterranean. *Are we actually in heaven?* Augustine asked himself. He did not know.

The bright afternoon faded into early evening, and still Augustine and Monica sat, awed by the experience they had shared.

"If only this day could last forever!" said Augustine. His taste of true wisdom had left him content as if he had devoured a banquet, yet he shivered in his yearning for more.

"No life will last forever on this earth," said Monica. She looked toward the sea, where the last faint colors of the sunset glimmered. "Son, for myself I have no longer any pleasure in anything in this life. Now that my hopes in this world are satisfied, I do not know what more I want here or why I am here.[8] God has given me everything I ever wanted: You are a Christian, and you have given up all to follow Him!" Monica's deep joy lifted Augustine anew.

"But now I am ready to go," she said impatiently as if she waited, baggage by her side, on the docks of Ostia for a ship to Africa.

I still need you, Augustine wanted to say. *Now that I am converted, I need you more than ever. And so does Adeodatus.* But he only could sit with a lump in his throat, overcome with love for his mother and longing for the eternal wisdom he had sampled.

"Why do I linger?" asked Monica. "Why am I still here?"

"We cannot go," said Augustine to the ship's messenger who informed him of the favorable winds. "My mother is not feeling well. And a voyage at this time would be very

91

unsafe." He knew that Maximus, a pagan general, had blockaded Roman harbors in an attempt to seize power. "We must await another ship."

Only a few days after their afternoon of spiritual ecstasy, Monica had contracted a fever and had remained in bed ever since. Alarmed, Augustine sent a message to Navigius, who was able to join their group in Ostia.

"I am so glad you came," said Augustine, hugging his brother.

"Of course, I came." The two sat together late into the night. Augustine slept a few hours, then entered his mother's room. Monica lay cold and white, her breathing labored and painful. She did not open her eyes.

"Call Navigius!" said Augustine sharply to the maid who had remained with his mother. He took her slender hand and prayed. *Oh, God, will You not grant me a few more years with her? I know she desires to go with You, but I cannot imagine life without her.*

All day the brothers sat with their mother, who had fallen into a coma. Adeodatus, his eyes round with fear, entered from time to time. Augustine felt himself growing drowsy and rose to walk outside in the crisp autumn air.

As he turned to go, Monica opened her eyes. "Where was I?"[9] she asked in an amused tone, as if she had lost her way coming back from the market.

Crying like little boys, Augustine and Navigius crowded together at her bedside.

Their grief moved her; she tried to reach up to soothe their tears. But Monica, as usual, was determined to have her say, even at the point of death. "Bury your mother here," she commanded.

"But surely you wish to die in your own country!" blurted Navigius. Augustine knew Monica had prepared a tomb next to that of her husband back in Thagaste and that she often worried that she might die abroad.

Now Monica sighed wearily. "Lay this body anywhere, and do not let the care of it be a trouble to you at all. Only this I ask: that you will remember me at the Lord's altar, wherever you are."[10]

"That we will always do, Mother," said Augustine fervently. She closed her eyes, exhausted, and drifted into a deep sleep, from which she did not wake.

Monica died at age fifty-six after an illness of nine days.

"Look, Augustine does not grieve," whispered one woman to another in the crowd that had accompanied Monica's body to the cemetery. "Perhaps they were at odds before her death."

Augustine stood beside her tomb, his face stern and dry. Adeodatus, his cheeks stained with telltale tears, tried to emulate his father's demeanor.

"I heard he sat and discussed the nature of the soul and other philosophies as they prepared her for burial," said the other.

"Then it is just as well that she is no longer in this world," said her companion.

Why do I feel so miserable, so abandoned? thought Augustine. *Plotinus considered those who mourn for loved ones irrational and ignorant. I myself believe that we should not weep and wail, as if she no longer exists. My mother is finally free of her suffering! And we know she is Christ's own. That is why I rebuked Adeodatus when he burst into tears at her passing.* Augustine prayed God would remove his pain, but the agony only intensified.

I deserted her back in Carthage, but she never deserted

me, thought Augustine. *During her illness, she expressed gratitude for such a faithful, caring son. Nothing I have ever done begins to match her love and her prayers for me. . . .*

After the funeral, Augustine could find no peace in prayer or meditation. He decided to go to the baths, as he had heard the Greeks claimed this would dispel worry and distress. But he found no relief. "This also I confess to thy mercy, 'O Father of the fatherless': I bathed and felt the same as I had done before. For the bitterness of my grief was not sweated from my heart."[11]

He went home and threw himself on his bed in desperation. When Augustine awakened refreshed some hours later, several lines of Ambrose's hymn came to his mind:

> *O God, Creator of us all,*
> *   Guiding the orbs celestial,*
> *Clothing the day with lovely light,*
> *   Appointing gracious sleep by night:*
> *Thy grace our wearied limbs restore*
> *   To strengthened labor, as before,*
> *And ease the grief of tired minds*
> *   From that deep torment which it finds.*[12]

Augustine recalled Monica's blanket-soft arms around him when, as a child, he sat on her lap. Memories of her hot, steaming bread on cold mornings, her gentleness when he was ill, her always-fervent prayers for him flowed through his mind and dissolved into a river of tears he could not stop. Augustine cried and cried. "It was a solace for me to weep in thy sight, for her and for myself, about her and about myself. Thus I set free the tears which before I repressed, that they might flow at will, spreading them out as a pillow beneath my heart. And it rested on them, for thy ears were near me—not those of a man, who would have made a scornful comment about my weeping. . .let him not laugh at me; but if he be a man of generous love, let him weep for my sins against thee, the Father of all the brethren of thy Christ."[13]

Monica's death so upset the thirty-three-year-old Augustine that he paid little attention to the fact that Maximus had tightened his blockade, preventing most ships from sailing.

"Let's go to Rome," he said to Alypius. Their hosts had urged them to stay, but Augustine needed to leave Ostia, where tender memories of Monica dogged his every step. "Let's go to Rome and teach there until this blockade is lifted."

"It will be good to see old friends before we go home," said Alypius. "Also, such connections in Rome may very well benefit us when we are living in a distant province."

"Hopefully, we will not have to wait too long," said Augustine. "Theodosius will never stand for such bullying by Maximus." Augustine had heard rumors that Theodosius, a Christian general who maintained the military rule of Constantinople, had already turned his troops toward Rome.

But Augustine, Alypius, Adeodatus, and Evodius were forced to stay in Rome for a year. Although still grieving deeply for Monica, Augustine focused on his work. He taught many who gladly welcomed the distinguished professor of rhetoric from Milan. He also began writing *De animae quantitate (On the Greatness of the Soul)* and *De moribus ecclesiae catholicae et de moribus Manichaeorum (On the Catholic and the Manichaean Ways of Life)*, his first major literary attempt to oppose his former faith. While his works still reflected his Neoplatonic views, he found himself more drawn to the Scriptures.

Late in 388 word came that the blockade was over.

"We're going home!" said Augustine. He had spent the past five years in the cultural capitals of the Roman Empire. Although convinced of his mission to Thagaste, he would miss the libraries, the intellectual circles, the cosmopolitan atmosphere of Italy. Once again Augustine's group made its way to Ostia. The breezes of the Mediterranean stirred his hair, his robe as he walked along the shore. How long before they carried him and his party far away to North Africa?

I wish you were going home with us, Mother, he thought. *But if not now, some day.*

nine

"Here they come!" called a young boy as Augustine and his group approached the main basilica in Carthage. "The *servi Dei* from Milan! They are coming!"

Several passers-by bowed respectfully.

Servants of God, thought Augustine. *Oh, Lord, may we indeed be Your faithful servants.*

While the *servi Dei* of the fourth and fifth centuries did not occupy official positions, the Catholic Church recognized and honored laymen who pursued a monastic life of contemplation and prayer. When Augustine and his party had arrived in Carthage, a wealthy Christian aristocrat had immediately offered them lodging. The bishop of Carthage would call on them today, bringing the prayer requests of faithful parishioners who entreated the prayers of the holy *servi Dei*.

How good it is to walk in Carthage again, thought Augustine. *But Adeodatus thinks it quite foreign. He recalled the harbor from which we departed, but does not remember the market where he and his friends played.*

"Look, Augustine! The lecture room where you first

taught me!" Alypius pointed.

Augustine laughed. "Was I ever surprised to see you! Your father and mine had an ongoing disagreement, and I never thought you would darken my door. But one day you came—"

"Just in time to hear your treatise against the circus games," said Alypius dryly. "I thought you had chosen your illustrations just for me!"

"Perhaps I did."

"At any rate, I rejoice that I no longer suffer from that addiction," said Alypius.

"As do I, old friend," said Augustine. "As do I." *He still struggles at times, as I do in remaining celibate. But God will help us.* Sometimes he marveled at the extent of Alypius's piety. The young man had completely turned his back on his former life. Once while they were in Italy, he chose to walk barefoot in the snow as a sign of his faith and dedication.

"How soon will we leave for Thagaste?" asked Adeodatus. He especially wanted to meet his grandmother's relatives, as he missed Monica deeply.

"In a few days," answered Augustine, "after we speak with the clergy here in Carthage." *Although the road is rugged,* he thought, *I am glad we will not be sailing again!*

"The light shimmers over the mountains of North Africa," said Augustine to his son, "as it does nowhere else. The 'daylight, that queen of the colors'[1] sifts down over the hills, the fields, the olive trees at Thagaste." A sudden longing seized him. "Soon we will arrive at home. Soon."

"Your kinsman Marcus seeks your aid in supporting his case," said the messenger. "He will meet with his opponent and the magistrate tomorrow in the early morning."

"I will be present," said Augustine, sighing. He had forgotten how readily North Africans sued each other. At Cassiciacum he had separated himself completely from everyday cares. Even in Milan, he had lived as a foreigner, with few ties to connect him to the concerns of others. But in Thagaste, where his family had lived for generations, all his relatives and friends were eager to secure the friendship and support of their kinsman, one of the *servi Dei*. Alypius, with his law background, enjoyed functioning in this capacity, but Augustine considered it a distraction that took him away from his study of the Scriptures.

But I am grateful for my family, God, Augustine prayed, *even if they demand my time and attention.* His sister, Perpetua, and her family as well as his other relatives had welcomed Adeodatus as their own, healing some of the boy's loss.

Thankfully, Adeodatus's mother has made no effort to contact us. Augustine had not expected any such communication, but the woman's evident resolve to continue their estrangement made it easier to adjust once more to life in Thagaste. Still, his heart and his flesh longed for her at times. . . .

Augustine, Alypius, Evodius, and Adeodatus lived in a small house on his father's modest estate. Only now did Augustine realize how much Monica's love had contributed to the well-being of the group. The men struggled to buy food, prepare simple meals, wash their clothes. His sister often sent her servants to help, but Augustine felt uneasy with women in the house, even his sister. Slowly the servants of God adjusted to their new way of life, training a male servant or two to share the load and helping each other perform the everyday tasks. Augustine had even learned to make bread using Monica's technique, as demonstrated by his sister.

But it will never taste as good as hers did. And no one can soothe the heart and mind with a smile, a touch, and a prayer as she did. No one.

"Alypius, I saw Justus and Sylvanus in the marketplace yesterday," said Augustine.

"Did you, indeed? How are they?"

"Totally deceived by the doctrines of the Manichaeans. Absolutely blinded to the insanity of their views!" Augustine's eyes filled with tears. "How could I have done it, Alypius? In my immaturity and my arrogance, how could I have swallowed strange doctrines that made God less than Himself? How could I have believed I was not responsible for my own sin? But I was not content to gulp poison myself; I had to poison all those around me! Forgive me, my friend; God forgive me!" Augustine wept bitterly as the trusting faces of his friends of his youth relentlessly flooded his mind.

Alypius clasped Augustine until he wearied of crying. "God has also used you to turn me to the right path," he said, "and Evodius, not to mention Adeodatus."

Augustine slowly nodded.

"He will use you to bring many more to Himself, using the gifts He has given you. Fight the Manichaeans, Augustine. Fight them with your voice and your pen. Their power prevails here far more than in Italy. Perhaps God has brought you here to rescue many who have naively welcomed their evil beliefs."

Augustine said nothing, but that night when Alypius found him asleep over his books, he read the title *De Genesi adversus Manicheos (On Genesis Against the Manichaeans)* at the top of his writing page.

"Augustine! You must come now!"

100

He glanced at his sister's face. "Many pardons," he told the city officials. "I must go."

"What's wrong?" he asked as they almost ran toward her home. "What is it?"

"Adeodatus," Perpetua gasped. "I've called for the physician—"

"What is wrong with Adeodatus?"

"He held his head, screaming in pain. Now he cannot speak. Oh, Augustine—"

Augustine charged madly into the house and clasped his son to his chest. But the beautiful dark eyes, so like his mother's, already stared glassily into space. The long, wiry young body lay like an image in Augustine's arms.

He is gone, gone. . .the only son of my body, gone. Augustine sank down holding the boy, hearing, seeing nothing.

Swirling shadows resisted the many-colored North African light and darkened Augustine's days. He and Adeodatus had carried on brilliant dialogues since their days at Cassiciacum. "His talent was a source of awe to me. And who but thou couldst be the worker of such marvels?"[2] Augustine had begun to compile their conversations in a book called *De Magistro (On the Teacher)*. "We took him for our companion, as if he were the same age in grace with ourselves."[3] Thrilled at his son's spiritual precocity, Augustine had pondered the boy's future. In Adeodatus's early death, Augustine had lost not only his precious son, but also a friend and close Christian brother of like mind. The little house of the *servi Dei* no longer echoed with Adeodatus's rapid, impulsive footsteps.

The gray mists that haunted Augustine did not soon disappear, for not long after Adeodatus's death at age twenty, Augustine's friend Nebridius also fell victim to an illness.

Even though he had chosen to live in Carthage rather than Thagaste when the friends returned to their native land, he and Augustine had continued a provocative, affectionate correspondence. "Your letters I have great pleasure in keeping as carefully as my own eyes. . . . They shall bring to my ear the voice of Christ, and the teaching of Plato and of Plotinus."[4] Augustine had reproved Nebridius because he seemed far more interested in Neoplatonic issues than Christian ones, but he missed Nebridius as if he were his own brother.

Oh, God, I know You Yourself are all I need. But spare me complete solitude, or I, too, shall die.

Alypius refused to let Augustine sink into the mire of self-pity. He spent more time than ever with his grieving friend, engaging his mind, pushing him toward public service, challenging him afresh to speak and write against the Manichaeans. During those months, Augustine wrote his treatise *De vera religione (On True Religion)*, a down-to-earth pamphlet that targeted educated, upper-class North Africans who toyed with Manichaeanism but had not yet committed themselves to the sect. He continued to work on his *De diversis quaestionibus octoginta tribus (On Eighty-Three Varied Questions)*, a book that answered inquiries various philosophers and theologians had made during Augustine's first years in North Africa.

Slowly the darkness lifted, and Augustine learned to rejoice that his son was safe at home with his true Father. Adeodatus rested in the family tomb where Monica was to have been buried. Augustine often visited the grave, standing silently before it, praying. *Adeodatus knew and loved You well.* Augustine wiped the tears from his eyes. *He was more Your child than mine. I need have no fear for him.*

"I believe I will go to Hippo Regius," Augustine told Alypius and Evodius at breakfast one morning. "A man named Olympas seeks to join a company such as ours. He is unable to visit Thagaste; therefore, I will to go him. I will also explore the possibility of opening a true monastery there in Hippo."

"If you think it advisable," said Evodius, "then go. What sort of man is Olympas?"

"Actually, he holds a position similar to yours when you were in the world," answered Augustine. "He is a member of the secret police, but senses the call of God in his life."

"I hope he will join us," said Alypius. He always welcomed any sign that Augustine was making plans for the future. "But take care, Augustine. Many towns are actively seeking bishops and priests. Clergymen in Numidia are circulating your writings throughout their congregations. Many have heard of you. If you show your face in Hippo's churches, they may well try to seize you for service."

"I know," said Augustine. "But Hippo already has a bishop, Valerius. I do not anticipate any complications in contacting him or appearing in the church."

"Very well. Go with God, my brother."

Later, Augustine's mule carried him gingerly down the steep slopes that bordered the Medjerda Valley to the coastal plain where the ancient city of Hippo Regius lay. *If bandits don't attack our caravan, and if this mule does not send me over these cliffs to heavenly glory first, we should reach the town before too long,* thought Augustine. How he hated traveling! *I suppose it is a characteristic of growing older,* he thought. *I am now thirty-seven years old. Perhaps adventure and I will part company at this point.*

He could not have been more wrong.

ten

Shall God's flock wander, afraid and helpless, without a shepherd?" demanded Valerius irritably in his heavily-accented Latin.

Why did the bishop of Rome appoint a Greek as a bishop in North Africa? thought Augustine impatiently. *Valerius can hardly speak Latin; and he certainly knows nothing of the Punic dialect spoken by many people here.*

"Shall they perish because none care for their souls?" railed the old man from his bishop's throne. "Shall they?"

Augustine fidgeted uncomfortably. He had not expected this outright recruitment of priests in the morning sermon. *Please, God, let him finish quickly. Even riding that stubborn mule back up the mountain seems preferable to listening to this endless sermon.*

Despite the winter day, waves of warmth swept through the church. Parishioners packed every nook and cranny of the basilica in Hippo. The sweating, restless congregation pressed Augustine on all sides. Mutters of assent rose from the crowd then grew into audible amens as their bishop spoke. Augustine edged closer to a pillar, but the throng flowed behind him, pushing him away from the door and closer to the front of the basilica.

Dear God, it cannot be!

"Augustine!" A voice behind him hissed in a whisper. Others took up the taut, breathy chant. "Au-gus-tine. Au-gus-tine."

"Augustine!" said the burly man in front of him. He turned to grin with white, ferocious teeth. "Augustine!" he roared. The people began to shout, and Augustine found himself helpless, carried by a flood of humanity toward the priests' benches and the bishop's throne.

"AU-GUS-TINE! AU-GUS-TINE!"

Do I seek to lead, Lord? No, I wish only to worship You in quiet contemplation!

The raucous crowd screamed his name, and the noblemen of Hippo gathered round to escort him to the altar. Augustine did not know if he felt more like a star performer or a prisoner about to be thrown to the lions in the Colosseum. *They did this to Ambrose,* he thought.

"God has shown us his priest!" said Valerius. His shrewd old eyes shone with gladness. "Do you agree to be God's servant, Augustine?"

Tears flowed down his cheeks, and he choked out, "I am always God's servant."

The church exploded in a mad cheer. The people roared his name as Augustine was consecrated at the altar.

"He is crying because he wanted to be acclaimed a bishop, not a lowly priest," said one man to another.

No, I am crying because I myself am a fool. I once jeered at priests and their congregations, and now God laughs at me. Now I, too, am a priest.

Valerius rubbed his hands with glee. The sun had set on this

Sunday evening, so he no longer fasted. "Bring my cup of warm wine," he commanded his servant. Valerius savored the day's events as he slowly sipped the spicy beverage. His elderly assistant, Adimantus, entered with noiseless steps and sat near the bishop as he always did after Sunday's flurry ended.

"We can rejoice, Adimantus," said Valerius. "God has provided a vigorous, gifted man to combat the Donatists and the Manichaeans. Catholics in Regius Hippo will once again prevail, and God will have a voice here."

Adimantus nodded. *If only I were younger,* he thought. *I could succeed Valerius and lead the Catholic Church in Hippo. But he is right. Our enemies are powerful, and we are a minority.*

The Donatists, Christians who emphasized strict purity in church members and clergy, refused to accept those who did not adhere to their stringent standards. No one could participate in the sacraments unless they were rebaptized according to Donatist tradition. Donatists rejected what they considered the unsanctified clergy of the Catholic churches and created their own church hierarchy. Wealthy North African aristocrats, both in the city and in the rich rural estates outside its walls, supported the Donatists. City officials bowed to their dictates. Once the Donatist bishop ordered the bakers of Hippo Regius to stop selling their delectable wares to Catholics.

"Remember when the Donatists closed the public ovens to Catholic use?" asked Adimantus. "They disrupted our neighborhoods; our women and children cried from hunger until we managed to change the city administrator's mind. What will the Donatists try next?"

"I don't know," said Valerius. "But this time they will find a worthy opponent in Augustine."

"He is not yet a bishop," Adimantus could not help saying.

"True." Valerius's sharp eyes searched his underling's face. "But he will do what I command him to do. Have no fear, Adimantus. I pray God will, in His mercy, grant me some years in which I can train Augustine. I am still the bishop. But there is no doubt in my mind that God has raised him up for these times."

"Then Valerius consented to our use of the church gardens for our monastery?" asked Alypius incredulously.

"Not only consented—he urged me to organize it as soon as possible," said Augustine. "He wants us to enlarge our group. I will be quite busy, as I began teaching the catechism classes almost immediately after I returned from my sabbatical. Thanks be to God that the bishop permitted me to pray and meditate on the Scriptures for some months after I was consecrated."

"I am glad he is using your true talents, not just relegating you to settling lawsuits and calming disputes."

"I still get plenty of that." Augustine frowned. "Only in the service of God would I consent to listen every day to such drivel." He folded his hands with a miserly gesture and whined, " 'Father, make my brother divide the inheritance with me!' No wonder Christ refused to waste His time in such a way! But I am His slave; I know such matters must be dealt with, especially among immature children." He sighed. "But Valerius says I will begin preaching in the morning services shortly."

Alypius stared. "It cannot be! No bishop allows a mere priest, let alone a new one, to speak during the mass."

"Illness plagues him often," said Augustine. "I will preach only to relieve his heavy burden."

107

"I have a feeling," said Alypius, grinning, "that Valerius will suffer an immense cold in his head—or a terrible sore throat—quite soon."

"Only God knows," said Augustine primly.

Augustine's catechism classes grew quickly. Young Christian intellectuals and ascetics throughout North Africa took notice of the new monastery. Valerius even hid Augustine when clergymen from other towns visited Regius Hippo, as he feared they might try to steal his priest. Both the Donatists and Manichaeans warily regarded the newcomer, the young priest whose polished, creative addresses moved people from all backgrounds as no one else had.

But the Donatists, like their Catholic brothers, viewed the Manichaeans as heretics who held far too much sway over the people. They even manipulated intellectuals with their smooth words and refined rhetorical style. When Valerius proposed a public debate in which Augustine, a former Manichaean, opposed one of their Elect, Fortunatus, the Donatists heartily agreed and joined the Catholic delegation in inviting them to compete. After all, the Donatists reasoned, Fortunatus could not possibly defeat the astute Augustine, the professional rhetor. If, by some bizarre chance, both contestants failed miserably, the Donatist cause was simply enhanced.

The first day of the competition arrived: August 28, A.D. 392. A huge crowd gathered at the Baths of Sossius, the largest intermingling of Catholics and Donatists Augustine had seen in Hippo. They rose and cheered at the sight of Augustine. He felt a surge of adrenaline. *I have not participated in a public debate since my conversion,* he thought. *God grant me a spirit of humility—but not weakness—in the face of the forces of evil.*

A large number of interested pagans also attended, many of them intellectual leaders in the community. *Perhaps, Lord, I can unchain their reason so they may find You.*

He stared Fortunatus squarely in the eyes. The Manichaean priest returned his gaze coolly. *Were we really once friends in Carthage?* Augustine pondered. *When I was a young Manichaean, I looked up to Fortunatus. Now I want to destroy everything he stands for.*

The Manichaeans, although a much smaller group, silenced hecklers with their air of mystical dignity. The white-faced priests, emaciated from their frequent fasting, led their followers in a stately procession into the large building.

Fortunatus welcomed their support. Although he showed no sign of nervousness, the leader of the Hippo Elect wished himself a thousand miles away. *I did not want this debate,* he told himself. *Who in his right mind would want to oppose Augustine? Even as a teenager, he was formidable. That is why he won so many converts for us! But the others of the Elect would give me no peace. I must do the best that I can. I must.*

Arcadius Augustus and Rufinus, the two consuls, seated themselves on thrones behind the debaters' positions and nodded. Both competitors turned and bowed. The rowdy throng quieted somewhat.

Augustine began: "I now regard as error what formerly I regarded as truth. . . . First of all I regard it as the height of error to believe that Almighty God, in whom is our one hope, is in any part either violable, or contaminable, or corruptible. . . . When you begin to expound. . .your system, we are compelled to declare Him corruptible, penetrable, contaminable. . . . I think it impious to believe that Almighty God ever feared any adverse race, or was under

109

necessity to precipitate us into afflictions."

Fortunatus answered, "Because I know that you have been in our midst, that is, have lived as an adherent among the Manichaeans, these are the principles of our faith. The matter now to be considered is our mode of living, the falsely alleged crimes for which we are maltreated."

Augustine answered, "I was among you, but faith and morals are different questions. I proposed to discuss faith." Augustine did not know if questionable practices had taken place during the meetings of the Elect, he stated, because he himself had been a mere Auditor, or Hearer, and was not permitted to attend such meetings. "But what you who are Elect do among yourselves, I have no means of knowing. . . . So keep the question about morals, if you please, for discussion among your Elect, if it can be discussed. You gave me a faith that I today disapprove. This I proposed to discuss. Let a response be made to my proposition."[1]

How could the omnipotent God, demanded Augustine, be threatened by a competing force of evil? Fortunatus ducked his question by pointing out the purity of the Manichaean community. When Augustine continued to question the dualism of Manichaeanism, Fortunatus insisted: "Truly it follows from the reason of things that there are two substances in this world which agree in forms and in names, of which one belongs to corporeal natures [the Evil], but the other is the eternal substance of the omnipotent Father, which we believe to be God's substance."[2]

Augustine declared that evil exists because man freely chose to sin, and that Jesus Christ, God's Son, came in the flesh to redeem mankind. The first day's debate broke up when Fortunatus opposed him: "This cannot be unless what is from spirit may be held to be spirit, so also what is from flesh may be known to be flesh. . . . 'Flesh and blood shall not inherit the kingdom of God, neither shall corruption inherit incorruption.' "[3]

"How dare he say such a thing! Jesus certainly did come in the flesh!" declared the Catholic and Donatist Christians, aghast.

"Was this not to be a debate based on reason, not the mindless quoting of Scriptures?" grumbled the pagans.

The audience's rumbling grew louder. The consuls called for a recess so the listeners could discuss in small groups what they had heard. This seemed to calm the throng, until Fortunatus stated that "the Word of God has been fettered in the race of darkness."[4] The halls of the baths almost vibrated with hostility. How dare Fortunatus blaspheme the Bible!

"Let us adjourn and continue the debate tomorrow," said the consul Rufinus hastily. The crowd reluctantly dispersed, although many left shaking their fists.

"We must procure a notary to record tomorrow's debate," said Arcadius Augustus. "Thus, we can give an accurate ruling if questioned as to the content."

"Excellent idea," said Rufinus.

The next day's contest brought even larger crowds and more noise.

"I say that God Almighty brings forth from Himself nothing evil, and that the things that are His remain incorrupt," began Fortunatus.[5]

Augustine answered, "And our faith is this, that God is not the progenitor of evil things, neither has He made any evil nature. But since both of us agree that God is incorruptible and incontaminable, it is the part of the prudent and faithful to consider: which faith is purer and worthier of the majesty of God?"[6] Is it the Manichaeans, Augustine asked, who say God "can be changed, violated, corrupted, fettered?"[7] Or is it Catholic Christianity, which insists God can "never be corrupted in any part, but that evils have their being by the voluntary sin of the soul, to which God gave free will."[8]

The debate raged on. Fortunatus asserted that when humans sin, they "are compelled by a substance contrary and hostile to ourselves."[9]

Augustine countered: "If the soul is commanded to repent, sin is from the soul, and the soul has sinned voluntarily."[10] *Oh, no, you don't, Fortunatus. You will not push that pernicious doctrine on these people. For years I refused to acknowledge that I myself was responsible for my sin, not some convenient ethereal "Evil."*

"It is perfectly plain, that repentance has been given after the Savior's advent, and. . .the soul can, as if washed in a divine fountain from the filth and vices. . .be restored to the kingdom of God whence it has gone forth," said Fortunatus.[11]

"Repentance? You speak of repentance?" asked Augustine. "Repentance is only possible if one takes responsibility for one's own sin. If this 'Evil' is the source of our sin, why should God command *us* to repent?"

Repeatedly Augustine hammered at the contradictory Manichaean assumptions that God cannot suffer injury, yet Evil can threaten Him. Augustine charged, wielding logic and wit like sharp twin swords. Fortunatus tried to stand his ground, but the Catholic priest's relentless attacks made him dizzy, especially as the throng made no effort to keep quiet but interrupted with constant hurrahs and catcalls.

"What then am I to say?" the frazzled Manichaean finally asked.

"I know that you have nothing to say," said Augustine, "and that I, when I was among you, never found anything to say on this question."

Fortunatus acceded: "When I shall have reconsidered

with my superiors the things that have been opposed by you, if they fail to respond to this question of mine. . .it will be in my contemplation (since I desire my soul to be liberated by an assured faith) to come to the investigation of this thing that you have proposed to me and that you promise you will show."

"Thanks be to God!" shouted Augustine.[12] Perhaps Fortunatus, too, would renounce Manichaeanism and return to the true faith.

"Thanks be to God!" echoed the thirsty mob. Most of them adjourned to wrangle the points of the debate over multiple cups of wine at the local taverns.

"Thanks be to God!" said the relieved consuls. The event had not degenerated into a total riot, and higher governmental authorities would not investigate them.

"Thanks be to God!" said Valerius fervently. His David had slain the first of the Hippo Catholic Church's many Goliaths.

eleven

I have written a new psalm against the Donatists," Augustine told the monks in his monastery.

"Please sing it to us!" said Evodius, who loved music. The others clamored to hear what they supposed was a highly spiritual statement of doctrine.

Instead, Augustine sang street-style Latin lyrics that told the history of the Donatist/Catholic schism, then called for Donatist repentance and reconciliation—all to a catchy tune that could have easily graced the marketplace. The monks listened, open-mouthed at such a common song, but soon hummed along. They laughed and applauded their leader loudly at the end.

"The Donatists still renounce the Catholics for accepting those who did not stand fast in their faith during Macarius's persecution," said Augustine seriously. "It is true many priests perished because they refused to hand over the Holy Scriptures to the infidels, and many Donatist families lost loved ones during that period of martyrdom. Their anger is understandable. However, that happened decades ago. They must not turn away God's people or demand they be baptized again. They must not refute the authority of Catholic churchmen because they are not perfect. The Church must remain unified and charitable. It welcomes not only saints but sinners."

Later Alypius said to his friend, "You won first prize twenty years ago for writing a classical *carmen theatricum.* Now you are writing vulgar popular songs for the masses?"

"Parmenian, the Donatist bishop of Carthage, composes songs against Catholics," said Augustine smoothly. "Why should I not use his own weapons against him?" He grinned wickedly. "Especially when I am so good at it. I only sing the refrain twenty times in all!" He bellowed out the chorus with glee.

"No one could forget this song if he had to!" said Alypius, covering his ears as Augustine continued singing. "The verses each begin with the next letter of the alphabet. The tune buzzes in my brain like an obnoxious fly. I will probably hear it in my sleep!"

"If it doesn't keep you awake."

In the coming months, Augustine heard gruff workmen, housewives baking bread at the neighborhood ovens, the monastery gardener, even children who ran in the streets, all singing his *Psalmus contra partem Donati (Psalm against the Donatists).* Alypius grew to tolerate its quirky rhythms. "At least the people are learning the truth."

Augustine had begun to preach regularly in the main basilica of Hippo. His congregation, poor and wealthy, educated and ignorant, stood rapt as he spoke in such a conversational tone they almost forgot they were in church. Despite Augustine's years in Italy, they considered him a fellow North African. He used vivid imagery that his audience understood, and he delighted them with his puns and wordplays. He told

115

jokes that made them laugh aloud, then moved them to moans and tears when he had to reprimand them. He talked without notes, except to read from the Scriptures. In Augustine's sermons, deep spiritual truths wore everyday clothes. Yet the pagan intellectuals, who could not resist attending the mass, found plenty of material for thought and discussion after the sermon.

While the Hippo congregations lauded Valerius's decision to allow Augustine to preach, the conservative bishops from areas around Hippo did not. Valerius ignored them. His churches now flourished, and he himself could rest more, as an elderly man should.

"Augustine, Aurelius has called for a council to be held here in Hippo—a first! Let us hope we bishops now will meet on a regular, not a random, basis as we have done for decades."

Augustine smiled. He had known Aurelius as a Carthaginian deacon for several years before the man had been appointed to the bishopric of the city in 392. Because Carthage was the chief city in the region, its bishop held authority over the other bishops in the area. *Aurelius certainly was never one to let the grass grow under his feet. He will guide us decisively, though prayerfully. It seems very natural to look to him for leadership.* Valerius's next words brought him out of his reverie with a start.

"Augustine, I wish for you to address the bishops at the General Council."

Augustine's jaw dropped. Was Valerius joking? The General Council of Africa established many important policies in the church. All the bishops of the region gathered to debate, affirm, and reject doctrinal stands. Augustine knew his prominence at this conference would arouse the ire of his opponents. "Are you sure, Your Holiness?"

"Absolutely," said Valerius. "Many of our bishops, while willing and worthy, are ignorant of the most basic Christian doctrines. You exhibit great ability in teaching groups with varied levels of understanding."

"If that is what you wish," answered Augustine.

So in October 393, Augustine found himself teaching a large group of church leaders who hailed not only from metropolitan areas such as Hippo and Carthage, but also from villages of Punic-speaking congregations far up in the mountains, isolated from Roman influence. Some of their priests boasted little more education than their flocks. They regarded the priest from Hippo suspiciously. *And several of the most powerful bishops have given me a rather cool reception,* thought Augustine. *I must take care not to undermine or threaten anyone's authority.*

He warned his listeners against groups of heretics who masqueraded as the church, especially the Manichaeans. The bishops began to listen with more respect; they knew Fortunatus, humiliated after the debate, had left Hippo forever. Augustine spoke on God's creation *ex nihilo* through Christ, the incarnation, the trinity, and the nature of the church. Later he summarized his sermons in a work called *De fide et symbolo (On Faith and the Creed)* that became a guide for Catholic churches.

Augustine, as always, spent many hours studying the Scriptures and writing. Before long he produced his first New Testament exegesis, *De sermone Domini in monte (On the Lord's Sermon on the Mount).* Augustine also had begun to write his *Enarrationes in Psalmos (Explanations of the Psalms),* a prodigious verse-by-verse analysis of all 150 psalms, which took the next twenty-five years to finish. Recognizing the importance of the Book of Genesis in his efforts to combat Manichaeanism, he attempted to

117

write another treatise on Genesis, *De Genesi ad litteram imperfectus liber (On the Literal Interpretation of Genesis, an Unfinished Book),* but left it incomplete until near the end of his life.

A year after the conference in Hippo, Aurelius called another conference in Carthage. Again, Augustine spoke to the bishops. This time he lectured on Paul's Epistle to the Romans; his talks were recorded in two commentaries. The same year, the prolific priest also completed a commentary on Galatians and a treatise on lying. But Augustine did not spend all his time in scholarly pursuits. His life as a priest kept him busy from dawn until late at night. People gathered by the hundreds to hear his sermons. His rapport with his parishioners grew each week—except when he spoke on sex and marriage. His congregation gave him polite attention, but none of them could visualize a life so spiritual that a person could love his enemies to the same extent as he enjoyed conjugal relations with his wife.

"Priests never understand these things," they told each other.

Augustine also stumbled into a hornet's nest when he opposed the *laetitia,* or celebrations on the anniversaries of martyrs' deaths. North Africans placed a great deal of emphasis on feasts at the gravesides of the dead. *Even Mother stopped baking her saints' bread only because Ambrose forbade it,* Augustine remembered. *But the laetitias go too far!* North Africans lit hundreds of candles and held processions on warm, sultry nights. Rhythmic music drew whole towns into sensual, crowded dances in the streets. Men and women alike conveniently forgot about marriage vows and sexual purity. Wine and hard liquor flowed freely, with most of Hippo's population dead drunk in honor of the saints.

How can they not see this is an excuse for license, not a religious experience?

Christians, Catholic and Donatist, saw no more inconsistency in this behavior than did the pagans in North Africa. Augustine wrote a passionate letter to Aurelius, urging his support of the boycott he wanted to implement. He received it.

Augustine preached against the *laetitia* the following Sunday. His congregation could not believe their ears. How could their beloved priest attack the most joyous (and numerous) holidays of the year, holidays their ancestors had freely celebrated before Christianity came to North Africa?

A woman near the front began to weep, then another. Tears flowed down the dusty, angry faces of the men. Weeping spread like an epidemic throughout the basilica. Even the small children knew something was wrong and bawled at the top of their lungs. Augustine cried, too, as he preached louder and faster: "Moved by the tears which they began to shed, I myself could not refrain from following their example."[1] In order to avoid being mobbed by the enraged, tearful congregation, Augustine decided to filibuster until the entire gathering was too drained to oppose him.

If all else fails, I will follow Ezekiel's example and tear my very robes in sorrow over their sin!

Augustine outlasted his weary congregation that day. He thought he had convinced them he was right about the *laetitias*. But he would battle the local culture for the next ten years in his efforts to outlaw the custom.

In a short time, Aurelius of Carthage became the most powerful churchman in North Africa. Augustine continued to cultivate his support. Aurelius took special interest in Augustine's monastery. He made sure Augustine had sufficient financial support to educate the earnest young men who arrived on his doorstep, eager to learn from the scholar whose writings circulated throughout the Roman Empire. They joined Augustine's familiar circle of friends: Alypius, Evodius, Profuturus, and Severus, all of whom had established ties with powerful Romans in Italy as well as the North African provinces. Alypius, with his ties to the imperial court, grew especially effective in gaining influence for the monastery. His link with Paulinus of Nola, a godly Christian Italian from one of the most ancient and wealthy families of the era, would impact Augustine's monastery both financially and spiritually. It metamorphosed into a seminary where North African young men became bishops, strong, godly leaders who served Christ within their provincial culture, and yet developed a broad worldview, as North African spiritual leaders had never before done.

By 395, Valerius had cleverly arranged for Augustine to take on the official role of bishop of Hippo Regius. Alypius was appointed bishop of Thagaste.

"You are leaving tomorrow?" asked Augustine as the two left the church after evening prayers.

"At dawn." For once, Alypius had little to say.

"So you leave me here alone with a congregation that uses astrology, amulets, dreams—and sometimes the Scriptures—to guide their lives; a bunch of monks, many of whom don't know Peter from Paul; and enough Donatists to populate Europe—except they all insist on living in Hippo!"

Alypius tried to grin. "At least you do not go to Thagaste, as I do, where every relative I have will immediately file a lawsuit and expect me to mediate on his behalf."

"You're a lawyer. You'll love it."

"Not nearly as much as I did when you lived in

Thagaste, too, Augustine. We've lived as brothers for twelve years. We've talked every day."

"I know." Augustine's throat tightened. *What will I do without Alypius, Lord? Only for You could I give up my best friend.* The two clasped each other in a strong embrace, tears pouring down their faces.

"Go with God, Alypius."

"Go with God, Augustine."

Soon Evodius was sent to Uzalis, and Profuturus and Severus, too, became bishops of neighboring towns. Together with Aurelius and the newcomers who eventually became bishops for other towns, they matured into a formidable religious and political circle of influence that not only permeated the North African countryside but expanded across the Mediterranean and throughout the western Roman Empire as well.

twelve

C ome sit with us, Your Holiness," said Linus, Augustine's monastery assistant. "The evening breeze blows directly from the ocean, and the garden is pleasant. The young men await your wisdom on many issues."

Augustine sighed; the fountain in the church courtyard gurgled its cool invitation. He tired of dealing with endless administrative tasks. A couple hours of pure theological enjoyment with his young students was definitely in order.

Augustine dismissed his stenographer with a grateful nod. *Thank God for my scribes! I could never accomplish so much without their dedicated help.* At times two or three secretaries worked together to take down his thoughts. Occasionally they took dictation from him late into the night. *God will surely reward such conscientious workers for their faithfulness.*

"Good evening," said Augustine. The monks, robed in simple black like himself, rose quickly to greet him. "Good evening, Your Holiness." How he missed his old friends, scattered far and wide in the service of God! But the young, earnest eyes now fixed on him brought a smile to his lips.

"Some of us still do not clearly understand Saint Paul's words in the fifth chapter of the Roman Epistle," said Possidius eagerly. "Would you please clarify what he means about sin entering the world through Adam?"

Augustine began to speak, and the students hung on his every word. *Much more than did my own son,* he thought with amusement. *Although Possidius does remind me of Adeodatus sometimes.*

Later, after the boys retired, Augustine sat by himself in the garden, drinking in the fragrant night air. *I did not know how simple, how blessed was the life of a monk when I was one! Rising early, praying long, serving in everyday tasks, spending hours in contemplation of God and His truth.* God in His wisdom, Augustine realized, had granted him several years for spiritual growth and development at Cassiciacum and Thagaste before he had been called to shoulder the heavy burdens of a parish priest and the heavier ones of a bishop.

Then again, the early months of my bishopric were unnecessarily complicated. Augustine frowned. Several area bishops had objected strenuously to his appointment. One, Megalius of Calama, a prominent bishop in Numidia, had refused to recognize his ordination for some time. Augustine was a Manichaean in sheep's clothing, he claimed. He also charged that Augustine had sent aphrodisiacs to an aristocratic married woman.

I did no such thing! fumed the bishop, digging his sandaled toes into the still-warm dust. *I sent a fragment of blessed bread to the wife of Paulinus of Nola. That is the extent of my love affair! So many are ready to accuse me about nothing. Even the tone of Paulinus's last letter seemed a bit cool because of that nonsense.*

Fortunately, the initial notoriety seemed to be dying; perhaps now Augustine could focus on other pressing matters. *I face plenty of challenging issues without the invention of imaginary ones to sap my energy.*

The spiritual management of only a few human beings in a monastery had mushroomed into the giant task of nurturing hundreds. Augustine sometimes quailed in the face of his responsibility before God to counsel, teach, preach, and administer the sacraments to so many. Intervention in their personal and legal squabbles devoured precious hours every day.

Augustine and his family were widely known and respected in Thagaste. But Hippo Regius, an ancient Roman city full of pagan reminders such as the huge theater, public baths, and a temple for Roman gods, did not always welcome an outsider, an upstart young Christian bishop. The Catholic church complex—adequate, but far from showy—hailed from the edge of town, not the traditional center of Hippo, where the pagan temple and forum stood. While Roman paganism no longer wielded the political power it possessed before Emperor Constantine became a Christian early in the fourth century, its influence still overshadowed Hippo in every way.

Donatist, not Catholic, beliefs dominated Hippo. The wealthy and the aristocratic of the city often maintained close Donatist ties because adherence to the church in power advanced them politically and economically. Catholics often intermarried with Donatists in hopes of gaining power. If a plaintiff wanted to win a lawsuit, he made sure the judges knew he was a Donatist. And if Donatist influence permeated the city's administrative and legal systems, it saturated the countryside outside Hippo's gates. The rich land barons had prudently remained

Donatists. Augustine quickly befriended them with his personal charm and sensitivity to their culture, but he knew if they encountered problems, they would seek out a Donatist priest or pagan official, not him.

And no landowner wanted to disturb his relations with the tenant farmers and other workers so essential to his lifestyle. Many people in the rural areas did not identify with Roman institutions, including the Catholic Church. Unbending Donatists for generations, they resented foreign ideas. Bands of wild, gypsy-like radical Donatists called Circumcellions roamed the countryside, conducting fervent banquets at the tombs of the martyrs and making random attacks on Catholic churches and villages, killing and burning as they went.

Catholic priests have learned to take safe, watered-down theological views, using their religious positions primarily to benefit themselves. Some of our bishops seem more pagan than the secular administrators; they waste their time turning church holdings into their own empires. Augustine felt like spitting in the dust.

Yet he had to admit that much depended on his ability to connect with influential people of many backgrounds. He often found himself sitting for hours, waiting to see a prominent nobleman. *This is worse than the imperial court in Milan!* he fumed. *It was so refreshing to cultivate the friendship of God and a few of His choice people during those quiet years in Cassiciacum and Thagaste. Now I must forge "friendships" in order to help my people and promote God's cause, whereas I normally would avoid such alliances. Satan tries to use that against me!* thought Augustine. *People say, "Well done! Excellent!" and unconsciously I try to earn their approval rather than that of God!* Later he wrote: "Certain offices in human society require the officeholder to be loved and feared of men. . . . In this way we come to take pleasure in being loved and feared, not for thy sake, but in thy stead."[1]

Augustine sighed and searched the diamond-studded night sky. Where could a tired, perplexed bishop go for true rest? He smiled and closed his eyes. "But see, O Lord, we are thy little flock. Possess us, stretch thy wings above us, and let us take refuge under them. Be thou our glory; let us be loved for thy sake, and let thy word be feared in us.[2]

"Emperor Honorius has defeated Count Gildo, Your Holiness!" said the messenger.

"Thanks be to God!" said Augustine fervently. Gildo, the Moorish military leader of North Africa, had tried to seize absolute power over his province in 398. Such a prospect concerned Augustine, as the count made no secret of his Donatist leanings. "And Gildo's friend, the Donatist bishop Opatus of Timgad?"

"Arrested, Your Holiness."

"But he is a man of great influence. While Gildo will, of course, be executed, I fear Opatus will gain his release. That must not happen. It *must* not."

Augustine sat down immediately and began writing another anti-Donatist pamphlet. He had authored many since his consecration as bishop, including *Contra epistulam Donati haeretici (Against the Letter of the Donatist Heretics)*.

Early in his ministry, Augustine had befriended the Donatist bishop Tyconius because of their common interest in the writings of Saint Paul. He met cordially with Fortunius of Tubursi, an elderly Donatist bishop, then told his colleagues they would be hard pressed to find as godly a bishop in their own ranks. He had occasionally offered to confer

126

with the Donatist bishops, assuring them of his peaceful intentions. However, most of the Donatists regarded such efforts with cynicism; they remembered all too well the Catholics' violent tactics in earlier times. In 304, Mensurius, the Catholic bishop of Carthage, and his deacon Caecilian had commanded an attack on a large group of supporters of Donatist prisoners. Their personal guards whipped and brutally beat the elderly parents and other relatives and friends who had brought food to their starving loved ones in jail. The food was thrown to the dogs. Another time, an entire Donatist congregation in a church in Carthage was massacred by imperial troops. With these memories, the Donatist bishops did not trust Augustine and his aggressive policies toward them. Later Petilian, Donatist bishop of Cirta, would denounce Catholic offers to parley, saying, "Thou wagest war with kisses."[3]

Now Augustine used every literary means possible to publicize the connection between Gildo, a man most citizens considered a traitor, and Opatus, a bishop who, recognizing the dangerous political climate, might simply have sought to keep peace. Augustine's efforts brought results.

"Opatus of Timgad has been executed!" Catholics in Hippo and Carthage lauded the downfall of the powerful Donatist bishop. Augustine's close friend Severus, Catholic bishop of Milevis, would take Opatus's place as spiritual leader to the new military leader appointed by Emperor Honorius.

After suppressing Gildo's rebellion, Honorius, a devout Catholic monarch, turned his attention to the paganism that still flourished everywhere in the Roman Empire. He decreed all pagan shrines be closed and sent government agents to North Africa in 399 to carry out his orders. They did not anticipate their reception. Enraged pagans assaulted the imperial representatives who called on the Roman forces in North Africa to defend them. Throngs of angry Catholics attacked pagan shrines on the huge landholdings of the wealthy; in a strange alliance, bands of Donatist Circumcellion joined them. Sixty Donatists and Catholics died in the town of Sufes, south of Carthage, in the riots.

Augustine and his fellow bishops mourned their deaths, but Augustine preached in triumph to immense Carthaginian crowds who celebrated the fall of paganism in their land.

"Down with the false gods! Down with the infidels who worship them!" they chanted. Catholics especially rejoiced, as in this victory over paganism, the emperor had made it abundantly clear that Catholicism alone claimed religious sovereignty in North Africa.

Augustine, who had feared the floggings from his teacher when he was a child in Thagaste and had trembled at the emperor's forces who threatened his mother's safety in Milan, found himself hurrahing with the mob at the violence done to the enemies of God.

"Why am I recounting such a tale of things to thee? Certainly not in order to acquaint thee with them through me; but, instead, that through them I may stir up my own love and the love of my readers toward thee, so that all may say, 'Great is the Lord and greatly to be praised.' I have said this before and will say it again: 'For love of thy love I do it.' "[4]

From 397 until 401 Augustine wrote a revolutionary book titled *Confessiones (Confessions)*, a long prayer that caught the attention of the entire Roman world. The Greeks had long employed the literary form Augustine used in his new book: that of addressing their philosophical questions to the Unknown God. Many past laymen and clerics had written accounts of their spiritual journeys, most of them concluding with the prospect of their own martyrdoms (the ancients would have regarded these as happily-ever-after endings). But Augustine's middle-aged, intimate autobiography eclipsed them all.

"Why is he pouring out his life story to the world? A bishop should not make such vulgar revelations public!" complained some of Augustine's fellow churchmen. "How can we maintain respect in our congregations if an eminent theologian opens himself like this? He says he still experiences sexual struggles, even as a bishop!"

But most readers understood Augustine's passionate honesty in revealing his youthful promiscuity and his past philosophical meanderings, as well as his contemporary battles with sin. "We lay bare our feelings before thee, that, through our confessing to thee our plight and thy mercies toward us, thou mayest go on to free us altogether."[5]

After all, Augustine thought, *Jesus Himself blessed the poor in spirit.*

"Why does Augustine allow his reasoning to be muddied by such intense personal feelings?" demanded some philosophical friends. "As always, he writes with excellent insight and style. But how will he perfect his character if he does not focus on philosophy alone?"

"I no longer cherish the delusion that I can somehow reach a higher level of spirituality by mere intellect," Augustine told his student monks in one of their garden sessions. "How I clung to that concept at Cassiciacum and Thagaste! But my life as a priest and bishop has changed all that. None of us can grow spiritually without God's help. As I told my dear friend Simplicianus, 'Work out your own salvation in fear and trembling: for it is God which worketh in you both to will and to do of his good pleasure' (Philippians 2:12–13).

"Only Christ can truly cleanse us and transform our lives," said Augustine. "Only He can help us delight in Him." He clasped the monks in his arms, then gazed deeply into each man's eyes. He sank to his knees in the late afternoon sunshine. The young men immediately knelt. "O Lord my God, my life, change my heart, change my actions, not only for my sake, but for the sake of the brothers I love so much," prayed Augustine.

Those who read *Confessions* heard Augustine speak of himself as a nursing baby, a rascally boy who gave in to peer pressure, an adolescent in love with love, a deluded young radical who dared defy his religious heritage—vivid portraits, interspersed with spiritual ponderings: Do babies sin when they cry for the breast? What caused the boy Augustine to steal pears he did not want? Should he have wept in grief at his mother's death? Exactly when does eating degenerate into gluttony?

In every philosophical discussion, in every anecdote of his *Confessions,* Augustine recounted God's relentless love for him, the perpetual prodigal son: "Belatedly I loved thee, O Beauty so ancient and so new, belatedly I loved thee. For see, thou wast within and I was without, and I sought thee. . . . Unlovely, I rushed heedlessly among the lovely things thou hast made. Thou wast with me, but I was not with thee. . . . Thou didst call and cry aloud, and didst force open my deafness. Thou didst gleam and shine, and didst chase away my blindness. . . . Now I pant for thee. I tasted, and now I hunger and thirst. Thou didst touch me, and I burned for thy peace."[6]

At the end of Augustine's life, when he examined all his works and made relentless corrections in his *Retractationes (Reconsiderations),* he felt the *Confessions* had stood the test of time. "My *Confessions*. . .are meant to excite men's minds and affections toward him. At least as far as I am concerned, this is what they did for me when they were being written and they still do this when read. What some people think of them is their own affair; but I do know that they have given pleasure to many of my brethren and still do."[7]

thirteen

A ugustine!" said Alypius hoarsely. "Augustine! They have attacked Cassius, our bishop in Bagai!"

"Who?" asked Augustine. "Who would assault God's servant?"

"His own Donatist congregation, that's who. When Cassius repented and joined the Catholics, they cursed him and dragged him from his church!"

Augustine closed his eyes. "Does he live?"

"Only because they did not torture him as efficiently as they thought."

Augustine's stomach lurched. Hot anger swelled in his veins and hammered his temples.

"When I heard the news, I immediately set out from Thagaste to tell you. Augustine, you must act decisively in this. You must, or such anarchy will destroy our church and our land." The keen eyes of Alypius the lawyer now superceded the gentle eyes of Alypius the provincial bishop.

Augustine winced. "The Donatists still charge us with oppression perpetuated by Count Macarius in years past," he said. "We cannot use strong military force against them as a group. I will urge the commander here to hunt down and punish the evildoers in that village. But I cannot demand the emperor's forces take universal action against the Donatists."

Alypius shook his head. "It must be done sooner or later, Augustine. If done sooner, fewer Catholic bishops and priests will be hacked like meat to be thrown to the dogs."

We've had this conversation before. Augustine sighed heavily. Alypius did not seem to understand his reluctance to advocate all-out military tactics.

Forcing the Donatists to abandon their beliefs would create other problems. Augustine already had to grapple with a huge influx of former pagans whose "conversions" to Christianity took place strictly for reasons of personal safety. They brought a host of heathen practices, such as feasting at gravesites, into the Catholic churches again, undoing Augustine's patient work of the past ten years. Could the churches also bear a flood of seething, embittered, legalistic Donatists who paradoxically expected to become intoxicated every saint's day?

But the treatment of the bishop of Bagai settled the controversy between the two friends. As soon as he had recovered sufficiently, the injured man petitioned the imperial court, charging the Donatists with brutality. Aghast, the emperor issued the radical Edicts of Unity in 405, which legally declared Donatists guilty of heresy and subject to all the penalties enforced on pagans.

The law, however, did not compel Donatists to become Catholics. It dissolved their hierarchical structure and stripped Donatist bishops and clergymen of their power. Catholic leaders confiscated Donatist church property. Congregations were dispersed, and the Donatist cause went largely underground in the cities.

133

"How can you persecute fellow Christians?" protested Donatist leaders. "The Scriptures say God granted free will to man to choose his spiritual fate. You believe that, too, if we read your writings against the Manichaeans correctly. How can you take that from us?"

Augustine replied that God had to discipline His wayward children as a father sometimes had to whip the son he loved in order to protect him. As a young priest, he had believed that his congregations, educated and sheltered from bad habits that fostered evil, would naturally progress from primitive spiritual levels to more advanced ones. Now, after ten years of ministry, he was convinced that most people would turn to God only because they feared Him.

Augustine also knew the number of Donatists rivaled that of Catholics in North Africa. Any compromise on his part might cause the weakening and destruction of Catholic churches.

"God is using the emperor's edicts to bring Donatists back to Himself," said Augustine. "If they truly love God, they will obey those laws."

Before the emperor handed down his Edicts of Unity, Augustine had already produced a mammoth collection of writings denouncing Donatism. He could not debate Petilian, Donatist bishop of Constantine, in person, but he made a vigorous case through their correspondence which became *Contra litteras Petiliani (Against the Letters of Petilian)*. He wrote similar treatises in his *Contra epistulam Parmeniani (Against the Letter of Parmenian)* and *Ad Cresconium grammaticum partis Donati (To Cresconius, a Donatist Grammarian)*.

He wrote a letter to his bishops, *Ad catholicos fratres (To Catholic Members of the Church),* which refuted the

Donatists' strong separatist views. Donatists believed they alone had preserved the purity of God's Scriptures; their spiritual forefathers had given their lives rather than handing God's laws over to persecutors to be burned, as some Catholic bishops had done. Augustine countered that God wanted His church to be truly "catholic" or universal. The true church, Augustine claimed, would never withdraw from the fellowship of other churches; such proud dissent did not promote Christ's righteousness or charity. For the first time in his writings, Augustine defended the use of force in maintaining societal order and in correcting the depraved behavior of its members. Many bishops used *Ad catholicos fratres* as a textbook to guide them in refuting Donatist challenges.

Augustine made additional detailed cases against Donatist re-baptism in his discourses *De baptismo (On Baptism),* and *De unico baptismo contra Petilianum (On the One Baptism against Petilian).*

I must take advantage of every opportunity in fighting this legalism, this defiance of God's authority, pledged Augustine. He debated the Donatists in person and in his writings at every chance he encountered. After working tirelessly to defeat Donatism, Augustine supported the severe measures imposed on its followers through the emperor's Edicts of Unity, hoping the Donatists would repent of their heresy and rejoin the true church.

Donatists no longer were permitted to hold public office or to pass down their sizable properties to their heirs. If Catholics challenged them in court, they could not defend their estates. Such impossible conditions caused most of the wealthy to abandon Donatist traditions and "embrace" Catholicism.

Augustine continually reminded his more vindictive

cohorts that Catholics were to act as instruments of God's instruction and grace, not revenge. As usual, he concocted his own methods of teaching the Donatists in Regius Hippo.

"Come with me, Possidius," said Augustine. He pointed to a pile of posters. "Carry these."

Possidius, who had come back to the monastery at Hippo for a few days of well-deserved rest, grinned ruefully. Augustine sometimes forgot Possidius was now bishop of Calama. He treated Possidius as if he were still the young monk who used to dog his steps in the church gardens. But Possidius did not mind losing a few years when he visited Augustine. He picked up the heavy bundle and trailed behind Hippo's bishop. "Where shall I take them, Your Holiness?"

"You will see." The two headed toward the main area of Hippo Regius and stopped in front of the grand Donatist basilica. Its windows were shuttered, its proud carved doors locked. Augustine produced two small hammers and gave one to Possidius. "Here. I will take this bundle, and you that. Tack these pages on that wall so the Donatists who persist in coming to their church read them." He himself began to hammer vigorously.

Street children, their eyes sparkling with curiosity, wandered over to watch the two bishops hard at work. Augustine teased them and permitted three boys to strike a blow or two. Then he began singing his *Psalm against the Donatists* to them. A couple of the children joined in. Before long, Augustine had the entire group singing the catchy song.

Possidius noted the posters contained Augustine's newest writings against Donatism. *So he has thought of a new way to publicize his views! His Holiness is a master at propagating his ideas to everyone, even street urchins.*

It took most of the morning to hang the posters. The noonday sun beat down on Possidius; his black robe clung to him, making him sweat even more.

"Finished!" said Augustine triumphantly. The children went home to eat, still singing.

"I wish everyone had a child's teachable heart," said Augustine. "I would far rather instruct with songs than with swords." He gave a sad smile. "Thank you, Possidius. Perhaps some Donatists will read these posters and return to the ways of God. If only my colleagues understood we are not to seek the deaths of the Donatists! We want them to repent, not to die forever in perdition."

Augustine exerted powerful influence over his own area of jurisdiction but could not persuade vengeance-hungry bishops who had suffered under Donatist domination to show them mercy. One imprisoned his Donatist counterpart for years and tried to arrange for his death. Others executed former Donatist leaders for past destruction of Catholic churches and the murders of their priests. Many estate owners who caught Circumcellions raiding their lands shrugged at the idea of reeducation, killing them on the spot.

"Why should we supply them with martyrs around whom they can rally?" asked Augustine. He protested the death penalty in a letter to the proconsul of Africa in 408 but made little headway.

Although the Donatist Church endured enormous pressures after the emperor's ruling, it did not die. Instead, Donatist priests and bishops fled from their cities and towns and took refuge in isolated rural areas, where most people still supported Donatism. The highly educated urban clergymen who had grown accustomed to soft beds, fine clothes, and elegant society found themselves living among wild, rough mountaineers who spoke Punic, not Latin. Under the leadership of outlawed churchmen, bands of Circumcellions continued their guerilla warfare, carrying their clubs they nicknamed "Israels," weapons to fight evil as they saw it. They whitewashed the "impure" walls of Catholic churches and demolished their altars. They also maimed and attacked Catholics, especially clergymen who dared travel in their domains.

Pagan influence still threatened Catholic believers. When Possidius tried to enforce the edicts, an angry mob attacked him while his congregation watched, unmoved by his plight.

"How could Possidius cause a riot?" cried Augustine in horror.

"He tried to halt a festival procession down the main street of Calama," answered Nectarius, a town official. He had come to Augustine to beg his help in deterring the Roman military from punishing the city for its unrest. "We have held such processions for generations. Most of us have forgotten they are pagan in origin."

"How is Possidius? Where is he?"

"Soldiers carried him to a small house well outside the city. The crowd trampled him; we were not sure he would regain consciousness, but the physicians believe he will recover."

"No one in the crowd defended him?" Possidius's eager face floated through his mind. *He so loves truth. He was always the first to leap into a discussion of the Scriptures.*

Nectarius paused.

"Where was his congregation?" Augustine's voice hardened, and he towered over the smaller man like a thundercloud, lightning shooting from his eyes. "Was there no one to speak even a word on his behalf?"

Nectarius cowered at the sight of the bishop's wrath. "Many in his own congregation believe he has interfered in our town celebrations once too often," he said finally. "I do not believe they really intended any harm. He threatened their way of life, the heritage of their hometown. You are from this area, Augustine. Surely you understand how we feel—our loyalty belongs to our towns, even above the love we feel for our parents."

Augustine glared at him. "If his loyalty to the heavenly city causes your city great difficulty, please forgive Possidius!" he said sarcastically.

"This incident *will* cause us great trouble," pleaded Nectarius, "if you do not use your influence on our behalf. I am here to offer our deepest apologies. My colleagues and I will do everything in our power to prevent another occurrence. What will you gain if the soldiers slaughter half the town? If our women and children suffer the deaths of their husbands and fathers?"

"I do not seek vengeance," said Augustine. "But I will not tolerate lawlessness and the ill treatment of my fellow bishops."

"Nor shall we," pressed Nectarius.

"Very well," said Augustine. "I will do what I can. But I make no promises. Your citizens may well suffer the terrible consequences of their folly."

"Thank you, Your Holiness." Nectarius bowed and left. Augustine watched him go. *Grant the city of Calama your mercy, Lord, in this world and the next.*

fourteen

Turmoil reigned during Augustine's middle years. Throughout his forties, the bishop and his supporters battled the Donatists in North Africa, who retaliated with guerilla warfare, both literal and literary. Vandals attacked Gaul in the far west. Rome itself struggled to defeat the invading Goths, a constant threat to the empire. Such unrest made it difficult to carry out everyday ministry, but Augustine enjoyed serving his people.

He also loved spending hours with his students and fellow clergymen at the monastery. Some monasteries were known for the gloomy atmosphere that pervaded their hallowed walls. But Augustine cultivated a more pleasant environment while maintaining order and propriety. Augustine did not tolerate the liberal views of some regarding the priesthood; he demanded his monks renounce their possessions, marriage, and other worldly pursuits. But his monastery, while stringent in its rules, gained a worldwide reputation as a center of learning where the educated or uneducated could read extensively, discuss, and pray with other students in quiet gardens. The fresh sea breezes not only cooled the blazing summer days; they also brought ships with news and letters from Rome, as well as constant international visitors who shared their views with those living in Augustine's house. Monks and visitors alike enjoyed their host's famous charismatic personality, his ready wit, his deep spiritual insights—especially at meals.

Augustine followed a strict vegetarian diet, except on his trips to Carthage. He frowned on intemperate eating and drinking. But everyone freely relished the rich discussions at his table. If an uneducated man made a good point, Augustine and his clergymen listened attentively. If an aristocrat stumbled in his logic, Augustine confronted him without hesitation. Dinners at the bishop's house were an education in themselves.

But Augustine monitored these meals closely. He decreed all would eat from common crockery but could use fine silverware, as he wanted diners to learn contentment under all circumstances. Those who swore lost their right to the one cup of wine allowed. He also abhorred gossip; Augustine wrote a poem on the table itself to remind them to watch their speech:

> *Whoever thinks that he is able,*
> *To nibble at the life of absent friends,*
> *Must know that he's unworthy of this table.*[1]

One day Leo, a visiting bishop from Gibba, brought news of a widowed owner of a large estate in his bishopric who had renounced remarriage in order to pursue spiritual truth.

"He has always been a generous donor but somewhat distant in his relations with the church. His wife was a pious woman whose lifelong devotion to the church was most admirable. His action surprised us, but we assumed

141

her influence had finally prevailed," said Leo.

Augustine sipped sparingly from his wine cup. His mind began a review of his latest pamphlet against the Donatists. A peal of raucous laughter drew his attention back quickly, as did Leo's next words:

"Who would have thought the sister of straitlaced old Felix would have been found in those circumstances! And *such* a beautiful woman! Why, he hardly has an ounce of flesh on his bones, whereas she—"

"She *what?*" asked Augustine witheringly. "Of whom do you speak?"

The dining room roared with silence.

"Why, Your Holiness, I speak of the sister of Felix, bishop of Cuicul," said Leo. "I just told you all: One of my priests visited the newly 'celibate' man in my congregation and found them in bed—"

"There is a spiritual application to this disgusting recital?" scowled Augustine.

"Certainly, Your Holiness. I, uh—"

"It had better be a good one, as neither Felix nor his sister is here to defend their family honor."

Leo stammered out something about sin.

"Sin," said Augustine, "can take many forms in many kinds of people. For example, there is the damnable sin of gossip." He slammed his wine cup down and threw his napkin aside. He pointed to the lines he had inscribed on the table: "Either erase that poem, or I shall go eat by myself in my room."

"There is no need for you to leave, Your Holiness," said Leo humbly. "I heartily repent of my careless words and will not trouble our company with more."

"See that you do not." Augustine looked around the table. "Does anyone wish to comment further on this story?

I recall you all found it immensely amusing."

No one answered.

Augustine's face suddenly broke into one of his charming smiles. "Perhaps Leo would like to lead prayers later on behalf of his sinful and needy parishioners."

"Certainly, Your Holiness," said the bishop quickly.

Augustine then raised a question about one of the psalms, and the pleasant murmur of conversation began once more.

"How are you, Perpetua?" Augustine smiled warmly.

His sister returned the smile. "We are all doing well, thank you." She automatically headed for the monastery garden, as she knew he would never invite her into the bishop's palace.

Perpetua usually enjoyed the opportunity to report to Augustine. He had appointed her prioress of his nunnery in Hippo after her husband died. As such, she was responsible for the atmosphere of serene piety and hard work expected of consecrated virgins. Although quieter in nature than her mother or brother, she had learned efficient management of people and resources during her years as a wife and mother. Rarely did she have to ask for her brother's intervention.

So she enjoyed their gentle talks in the garden. Occasionally Augustine's teasing grin brought back memories of her mischievous little brother's tricks. Sometimes Augustine even forgot he was now a bishop. But not often. And he never forgot Perpetua was a woman.

Although he appreciated her devotion to Christ, it had not occurred to him that she, too, had inherited their parents' keen intelligence. She caught snatches of his learned discussions with the monks, cherished his sermons, asked questions he willingly answered—because they were the questions allowed a woman. Augustine had once written that women's chief function was to produce children—otherwise, why did God create them? But unlike many of his contemporaries, he treated women, poor and rich alike, with courtesy and respect. Augustine often wrote to devout ladies of high birth, giving them spiritual counsel; he considered them his good friends.

As long as they maintained their distance.

"Letters, Your Holiness," said Linus. "This morning's ship brought one from Jerome of Bethlehem, and couriers brought letters from Evodius and Alypius as well!"

Augustine smiled, then picked up Jerome's letter with a sigh. *Business before pleasure,* he told himself. He wished he and the eminent theologian could be better friends.

Augustine had first sent a letter to Jerome requesting important Greek commentaries that had been translated into Latin. Jerome chose to ignore it because he no longer regarded Origen, the chief author of these, as a valid Christian authority. From that moment, the two bishops locked horns like mountain goats staking out their territories. Augustine knew his youth and aggressive intellect threatened the man. Jerome possessed an unswerving instinct for making Augustine feel provincial and ignorant. Both spoke of their personal humility and Christian charity; then each immediately offended the other. Augustine paced back and forth as he dictated a civil—but not too civil—reply to courteous lines that shouted insults. "Please give this immediately to the courier," said Augustine. He could not get it off his desk fast enough.

Thanks be to God that Paulinus of Nola and I have a better relationship, thought Augustine. *Now that he no longer believes those stupid rumors my enemies spread about his wife and me when I first became a priest, we can*

*enjoy our intellectual equality and spiritual brotherhood.
At least we can enjoy our friendship as much as any who
converse only through letters.* Despite his desire to meet his
famous correspondent in person, Augustine never did. That
he never met Jerome disturbed him less.

The letters from Alypius and Evodius caught his eye,
and he opened them eagerly. *How I miss my dear friends!*
He loved the earnest young monks who hung on his every
word, and he enjoyed the abiding love and respect of his
congregation. But Augustine and his friends had all sacrificed their close-knit circle to minister as bishops in Hippo
and the surrounding towns.

"When your own time comes to surrender to the claims
of churches in remote places some of those whom you have
educated, and who are most dear and sweet to you, then, and
not till then, will you know the pangs of longing which
pierce me through and through for some who, once united to
me in the strongest and most pleasing intimacy, are no more
beside me," Augustine wrote to a younger colleague.[2]

Even a few miles of travel presented a challenge in time,
energy, and safety, as the rugged Numidian terrain and
uncertain weather made journeys difficult. The ever-present
threat of attack by the Circumcellions or common bandits
discouraged most trips. But Alypius, Evodius, Severus, Possidius, and Profuturus usually managed to meet Augustine
in Hippo on their way to the bishops' conferences that
Aurelius, the primate or most prominent bishop of North
Africa, called almost every year in Carthage. The comrades
savored these rare times in which they could shed their
responsibilities and simply travel as friends. They told theological jokes no one else understood and challenged each
other with number puzzles and riddles from the Scriptures. They mimicked each other's sermon styles and teased

each other about their pasts. Augustine might be their leader, but Alypius never let him forget he had once skipped town in the middle of the night to escape his mother. They spent long, fruitful hours in discussion and prayer together, often unburdening their souls on issues they could never reveal to their congregations. *We yearn to see each other more often, but somehow it cannot happen.*

Alypius's letter began with a jocular greeting but quickly listed several complications that concerned him in his congregation: a lawsuit in which a groom's family sued the bride's because she had decided to become a nun; a monk who had secretly retained his inheritance; an itinerant Donatist who preached in small villages around Thagaste, inflaming the people. He also pointed out a flaw in Augustine's last treatise.

So Alypius is the expert now on Paul's epistles? Augustine's brows knit together, and he frowned, then laughed at himself. *Alypius is correct, of course. He spotted my inconsistency immediately. One becomes accustomed to the praise of everyone. Only those who love me completely possess the courage to tell me I am wrong.*

The rest of Alypius's letter bulged with financial and legal details. "I am sorry to babble on about trivialities," wrote Alypius. "I know they do not interest you, as they do me. But together we must solve such problems before they grow into big ones."

I know, dear friend, I know, sighed Augustine. *But some day we will have all eternity in which to hold our conversations, and they will concern only God Himself, not the pitiful earthly concerns that gobble up our letters and our time together.*

" 'Whosoever shall say to his brother, Thou fool, shall be

in danger of hell fire,' read Augustine to his congregation. "Yet 'the tongue can no man tame.' Man tames the wild beast, yet he tames not his tongue; he tames the lion, yet he bridles not his own speech; he tames all else, yet he tames not himself."[3]

Augustine spoke, as always, from the bishop's throne, the *cathedra,* on a raised platform. His people stood patiently, sometimes for hours, men on one side of the basilica, women and small children on the other. When his words were not to their liking, they grew restless and even complained audibly. But most of the time Augustine's sermons captivated them, and they cheered him in true North African tradition.

"No one can preach like our bishop," they bragged to friends who suffered the usual three-hour sermons from less gifted speakers. Who else but Augustine would build his sermon around the animals they saw every day in their stables and (unfortunately, Augustine would say) at the games: "The horse does not tame himself; the camel does not tame himself; the elephant does not tame himself; the viper does not tame himself; the lion does not tame himself; and so also man does not tame himself. But that the horse, and ox, and camel, and elephant, and lion and viper, may be tamed, man is sought for." Augustine paused, then thundered, "Therefore, let God be sought to, that man may be tamed!"[4]

Preaching from Scripture passages that spoke of the security of believers under the wings of Christ, Augustine spoke of the "Hen of the Gospel," the gentle mother who viciously attacked those who would threaten her little chicks.[5] He likened hope to an egg; a fish to faith; a scorpion, with its poisonous tail, to Satan—Augustine used any imagery he could to enforce the lesson to a congregation that included those who could not sign their names as well as those who could quote Cicero.

Augustine rarely took a vacation from preaching. Congregations in Carthage often requested that he speak. When he visited other cities and villages, the bishops, in response to their flocks' demands, always asked him to give the homily. Sometimes he preached several times on a Sunday.

Augustine felt an immense responsibility to God and His people when he taught. His words, he knew, guided the congregation's eternal destiny. God had entrusted their very souls to his care, and he trembled in awe of that assignment.

But he also loved to preach. His education had revolved around rhetoric, and his sermons presented continual opportunities to exercise the gifts God had given him. Oratory had not always held a high place in the mass before Augustine; his famous sermons changed that view in many churches.

Augustine also never stopped writing. Besides treatises against Donatism, he also had produced a wealth of works debating the Manichaeans. He continued to fight pagan influence in his essay *Quaestiones expositae contra paganos VI (Six Questions against Pagans),* written in A.D. 408. *De doctrina Christiana (On Christian Teaching)* outlined his method of preaching and the centrality of Scripture in sermons. Augustine began his monumental work *De Trinitate (The Trinity)* to combat the view of the Arians, who believed Jesus Christ was inferior to God the Father, and those of other sects who did not recognize the validity of the trinity. He did not finish either of these works until late in life.

Sometimes theological students and clergymen refused to wait for the completion of his books and pamphlets.

"This is but a first draft of my book!" said Augustine to a group of visiting clergymen. "Where did you obtain this copy?"

"My apologies," said one bishop. "We had no idea some-one had taken it without your permission. I bought this from a bookseller in Carthage, who assured me it was your latest. Of course, I wanted to be the first to read it, and I have shared it with my colleagues."

Augustine shook his head in irritation. "If people demand accurate scriptural answers to their questions, they must let me finish my books!" He gave a rueful smile. "At least they are interested in the things of God."

Clergymen and lay people throughout North Africa and across the Mediterranean took interest in what Augustine had to say about the things of God. Sometimes he answered their questions about the Bible, as in *Quaestiones evangeliorum (Questions on the Gospels)* and *Questionaes XVI in Matthaeum (Sixteen Questions on Matthew),* both written from 399 to 400. Augustine discussed creation, temptation, the Fall, and Paradise in one of his most famous commentaries *De Genesi ad litteram (On the Literal Interpretation of Genesis),* begun about 401. He also started a long collection of sermons on the Gospel of John during this period and wrote a commentary on the Book of Job. He dictated treatises on marriage, fasting, demons, monastic life—Augustine routinely juggled the creation of several literary works.

"Augustine, you need more sleep," said Alypius. "You'll tire yourself out completely and become even more ill if you don't take care of yourself."

A coughing spell kept Augustine from answering for a few minutes. He gave a weary smile. "I know. But the people need answers, they need counsel, they need advocacy in their lawsuits and intervention with the authorities—"

"They need you, Augustine. They will lose you if you do not listen to me."

"Sometimes I wish I could live a life of seclusion and contemplation like Paulinus of Nola. But I know God has called me to serve the people." Before Alypius could protest, Augustine agreed. "I will go to the country this winter."

True to his word, he stayed at a friend's villa not far from Hippo that winter. In the years after their conversation, Augustine took occasional retreats to rest.

But not for long.

I have a good life in Your service, Lord. A busy life, a strenuous life, but a good one.

Augustine was enjoying a rare moment of complete solitude during the busy summer of 410. He had arrived in Carthage the day before and did not anticipate his usual morning of legal wranglings in Hippo. Augustine had risen well before dawn to pray and now luxuriated in the freshness of the August morning. He intoned:

> *Blessed is the man that walketh not in the coun-*
> *sel of the ungodly, nor standeth in the way of sin-*
> *ners, nor sitteth in the seat of the scornful. But his*
> *delight is in the law of the LORD; and in his law*
> *doth he meditate day and night. And he shall be like*
> *a tree planted by the rivers of water, that bringeth*
> *forth his fruit in his season; his leaf also shall not*
> *wither; and whatsoever he doeth shall prosper.*
>
> Psalm 1:1–3

"Your Holiness, Your Holiness!"

Linus's high voice assaulted the gentle silence. *What*

can it be? One look at his assistant's face quelled his annoyance. "Yes, Linus?"

"Alaric has sacked Rome! The Visigoths have set fire to the city!"

It was as if Linus had told him the sun had plunged to the earth, leaving the sky in blackness, setting the world ablaze.

Augustine fell to his knees.

fifteen

T he consuls in Carthage have lifted the laws against Donatism," said Aurelius a few months later.

Augustine stared at him, open-mouthed. "But how?" he finally asked. "How can they ignore the edict of the emperor? Why did they do such a thing?"

"Right now the emperor cannot afford to fuss over North Africa," said Aurelius. "He must gather together all his armies in an attempt to chase Alaric out of Italy. Thanks be to God that the Visigoths have not captured Ravenna, where the imperial government now dwells. But the authorities here in Carthage realize they cannot enforce the emperor's edict without his military assistance. They consider their ruling diplomacy that will calm the hostilities between Catholics and Donatists in our provinces—at least for a short while."

"It will do exactly the opposite," said Augustine firmly.

The coming months confirmed his worst fears. Not only did the local officials nullify the laws against the Donatists, but the Catholic emperor, Honorius, suspended his Edicts of Unity for a year. The Donatist bishop, whom

Augustine had all but chased out of town, rode back into Hippo followed by hundreds of cheering Donatist supporters. Now wary of the "converted" Donatists in their congregations, Catholic believers began shunning them in business and social situations. The Donatists welcomed these ostracized members back with open arms. The underground church that had languished since 405 now rose like a phoenix from its ashes to swoop down upon its enemies, the Catholics, who huddled within their homes like a people under siege. Catholic clergyman began to fear for their lives.

"Your Holiness, I beg you not to travel right now." Linus's forehead wrinkled in concern. "As long as you stay in the bishop's house or appear in public places, I don't believe the Donatists would dare attack you. You have too many supporters. But if you leave the city walls, they may make an attempt on your life."

"I am well aware of their evil thoughts," said Augustine. He continued packing. "But it is essential that I make this trip to Rusicade. The bishop there quails before the Donatists. If I do not strengthen him and his people, they may give in to threats and blackmail." He smiled at the young man's concern. "It is not far. Have no fear for me, Linus. God is with me."

"I would worry less if your regular guide accompanied you," said Linus.

Inwardly Augustine agreed, but he tried hard not to show his anxiety. "Demetrius is ill and cannot go. His kinsman Phoebus has agreed to guide me to Rusicade. Although young, he is said to be trustworthy."

"I hope so," said Linus. "I will pray for you night and day until you return," he vowed solemnly.

Although well-intentioned, Phoebus guided the party

along the wrong road through the rugged mountains, nearly doubling their travel time. Augustine arrived, exhausted and nearly ill. Once he returned to Hippo, he vowed, he would never so much as go to the marketplace with Phoebus! But upon reaching his home, the bishop learned that their misdirected travels had saved his life.

"The Circumcellion plotted to kill you!" said Linus, throwing his arms around Augustine.

"I know. But because of your prayers, they failed," Augustine assured him. The other monks gathered around him; he tried to hug them all at once.

"We heard they lay in wait along the main road to Rusicade!" said one.

"Even now you could be lying dead up in the mountains," said another.

"Through Phoebus's mistake, God preserved your life," said Linus thankfully. "Your Holiness, you must even now use extra caution; the Donatist leaders are incensed and humiliated. Who knows what they will do?"

Incensed himself, Augustine lashed out at the Donatists: "You do not frighten me! God sits on His throne, not a Donatist! With His help, I will continue to seek the lost sheep, as my Shepherd does, in the mountains of peril or the valley of death!"

Donatists and Catholics continued their civil war until Emperor Honorius called for a meeting, a *Collatio,* in 411, in which the bishops of both churches would present their cases before Flavius Marcellinus, an imperial officer and a fervent Catholic.

"Thanks be to God for the emperor!" said Augustine as he hugged Alypius. "North Africa cannot continue like this. We Catholics have long craved this opportunity for official recognition and acceptance throughout the land.

Now the emperor gives it to us."

"So you think this trial will convince the Donatists?" asked Alypius with a wry smile.

"Of course not! At least no *collatio* on earth will convince the Donatist leaders. But our case may persuade the many who do not completely understand the spiritual differences between us. It will also clarify the legal aspects of the situation."

"Now you sound like a lawyer," said Alypius, grinning. Then he turned serious once more. "Do not underestimate the Donatists, Augustine. They will, no doubt, appeal to popular opinion at the trial. They will count on their numbers and the influence they have maintained in North Africa for decades. No wonder they increase! They invite our more shallow converts to celebrate the *laetitias*. Their membership swells daily, it seems."

"I, of all people, will never underestimate the Donatists!" said Augustine. "But public opinion does not change the facts of the case. Nor will it move Flavius Marcellinus. He is a man of immense integrity. He knows the law. Even if he were not Catholic, I would have great confidence in his ability to render a just decision. Perhaps this will not be so difficult, Alypius."

"I hope you are right."

"They are coming! They are coming!"

The cry went up in the marketplace of Carthage on the beautiful May morning. Men paused in their conversations about the price of olive oil and the latest circus games. Women stopped gossiping and gathered their little ones close to them. Adolescent boys ran to see what had caused the commotion at the city gates, beggars slinking close behind.

155

A slow, splendid procession wound into the city. Two hundred eighty-four Donatist bishops from every corner of civilized North Africa rode silently, two by two, on enormous, spirited horses who tossed their heads proudly. Most of the Donatist bishops bore the marks of hunger and suffering from living as outlaws, but they had procured the best clothes they could for this *Collatio* that would determine their destiny and perhaps even their survival. Dressed in shabby but brilliantly colored capes embroidered with Christian symbols, they marched, heads held high, past the awestruck crowds who parted for them like the Red Sea before Moses. Petilian of Constantine led them all, his face glowing like a sunrise, his black eyes full of fire, empty of compromise.

Augustine watched the imposing parade from afar. He wore his usual simple black robe and walked the streets of Carthage that day with little fanfare. But his hard gaze reflected Petilian's resolve.

"The Catholics assert they are the true church," said Petilian. "But are they? Have they presented evidence which confirms that statement? Do they not bear the name of Jesus Christ in vain? They are the plaintiffs in this trial; they must substantiate their accusations. We accuse no one. As our Master once did, we now stand before Pilate, guilty only of loving our God."

Marcellinus, the imperial commissioner, stood as he had stood throughout two earlier day-long sessions. Normally, he and the rest of the court would have seated themselves at the trial's onset. But all 277 other Donatist bishops stood at attention behind their seven invited leaders to grimly observe the proceedings. The Catholics, not to be outdone, had lined up a delegation of their own. Marcellinus, a conscientious, reverent layman, could not sit down while the

Lord's bishops stood on their feet. So the weary but patient commissioner stood also, listening to Petilian's presentation. Sweat dripped from his face as the ancient baths, packed to the roof, grew uncomfortably warm.

Petilian hammered at Catholic theological positions, as he had for the past two days. The first day he had also charged that the Catholics could not muster sufficient support for their cause. "Does not their little group pale in significance to that of God's true church?" he asked with a smile. "They list bishoprics on their roster where, in fact, they have no presence at all."

Furious, the Catholics had conducted a roll call of bishops in the Carthage marketplace to fight Petilian's accusation. But the Donatist bishops again assembled en masse to challenge their opponents. Arguments broke out as opposing bishops from the same town shook their fists at each other. As names were called, the rivals recalled the ugly injustices suffered at the hands of the other:

"Tullius should have no problem identifying me. He would have loved to kill me but contented himself with throwing me into prison and threatening my family!"

"Titus kidnapped my niece, thinking he could force me into renouncing my faith!"

The roll call nearly became a riot.

The Donatists then won a delay of the trial because, they claimed, they wanted to examine the stenographer's records of the earlier proceedings. "Why not?" asked Augustine, in his first brief speech of the trial.

Possidius, who was standing near his mentor, scowled. *Alypius and I have done more than our part already. But Augustine has said nothing.*

"By all means, let them take all the time they need," said Augustine.

157

"Your Holiness, why would you agree to such a thing?" asked Possidius later. His eyes still glinted with the heat of the contest. "Should we not resolve this issue for the sake of the people?" In the passion of debate, Possidius had peppered his rhetoric with insults. He faced his mentor impatiently. "Why do you not put forth our cause?"

The other bishops stared at him, open-mouthed. *So, Augustine,* thought Alypius. *Behold yourself in a younger form!*

"Patience, my son," answered Augustine. "Their delay will only hurt their case. I promise you, I will speak soon."

Both Donatists and Catholics had welcomed a break from the long, miserable days in the baths, as did Marcellinus, who spent much of his unexpected free time in prayer and meditation. The court reassembled five days later, refreshed and ready to resolve the issue.

But the hot day once again turned the baths into a steaming purgatory. The proceedings dragged on listlessly while Petilian rehashed points he had made at least once before.

Then Augustine rose.

Speaking without notes, he held the room spellbound as he dismantled the Donatist case, which was based largely on theology.

"Your Holiness, I have great regard for your spiritual reasoning," said Marcellinus respectfully. "But I am no bishop, and I certainly cannot define or refute theological views. The emperor simply wishes me to explore the legal support for the preeminence of one party over the other."

"I completely understand your position," said Augustine smoothly. "I bring before you a collection of documents which, I believe, will substantiate the claim of the Catholic Church as the true church of the Roman Empire, and thus the true church in North Africa."

Marcellinus's eyes lit up. At last, something tangible a precise Roman bureaucrat could review and evaluate!

"Emperor Constantine himself ruled on this question almost a century ago," Augustine proclaimed. "When the Catholics and the Donatists first separated, the Donatists—not the Catholics!—asked him to decide which would be the official church. He did so. He declared the Catholic Church to be the true church of the Roman Empire."

Augustine wiped his forehead and looked around the unbearably hot courtroom. "Yet, after such a precedent, we have spent days in fruitless debate and useless review, listening to endless drivel that bears no relevance to the real issue: Did or did not Emperor Constantine make such a ruling? The documents we submit say that he did." With that, Augustine sat down.

The hum of conversation in the public baths quickly escalated into an angry buzz. The Donatists searched each other's faces, looking for optimism.

Marcellinus quieted the crowd. "I will examine these," he said shortly, "and summon you when I am ready to deliver a judgment." Evidently Marcellinus felt the trial had wasted enough time and energy. In the wee hours of the next morning, he sent messengers to the leading bishops of the Catholic and Donatist delegations and summoned them once more to the now-deserted public baths. "The documents support the Catholic claim to be the official church," said Marcellinus. He stared at Petilian and the Donatist bishops. "In the name of the emperor, cease your attempts to mask the truth!"

When Emperor Honorius had issued his Edicts of Unity, the Donatist Church simply had been dissolved. Now, after

Marcellinus's ruling, the imperial government's representatives actively persecuted Donatists. They considered themselves to be instruments of God, as well as servants of their emperor. Laymen who refused to convert to Catholicism paid exorbitant fines. Once more, a Donatist could not pass on his inheritance or hold office. If Donatist bishops persisted in their religious activities, they were hunted down and imprisoned, even executed. Former members of their congregations feared to offer them sanctuary.

Such an atmosphere bred a dark despair among the Donatists. Gaudentius, the Donatist bishop of Timgad, had been one of the wealthiest and most powerful men in Numidia. As imperial agents approached the city, he barricaded himself and most of his congregation in his magnificent church and threatened to burn it down before surrendering to his oppressors. The Circumcellion, who had lost their leadership in losing their bishops, seemed to have lost their heart also. No longer funded by wealthy supporters, they suffered deeply; a rash of suicides broke out among them.

Although such actions saddened Augustine, he did not alter his views. Neither did he back away from influencing the imperial agents to do what he saw as their duty. The Donatists had disregarded the laws of God and man. They must pay the consequences.

sixteen

W hat will we do with all these immigrants?" Linus threw his hands up in despair. "They arrive daily from Rome; they have nothing! They need food, clothing, and lodging. Where will we get the money for all this?"

"God and His people will provide for the destitute," said Augustine. "Even the poorest members of our congregation do not hesitate to help a stranger. And you forget, Linus, many 'refugees' bring enormous wealth with them. Noble Christian families are coming to their estates in North Africa until Rome can be secured. Many are true followers of Christ and have been most generous with their money in Italy; I am sure they intend to practice charity here."

Albina, her daughter Melania, and son-in-law Pinianus, devout aristocrats from Rome, had just arrived in Thagaste, to the delight of the townspeople. Two years had passed since the fall of Rome in 410, and the young couple had sold their immense landholdings in Italy and given much of the money to the poor.

Augustine wrote to them, welcoming them to North

161

Africa and apologizing because he could not leave his church to visit: "The congregation of Hippo, whom the Lord has ordained me to serve, is in great measure. . .of a constitution so infirm, that the pressure of even a comparatively light affliction might seriously endanger its well-being; at present, however, it is smitten with tribulation so overwhelming, that, even were it strong, it could scarcely survive the imposition of the burden. Moreover, when I returned to it recently, I found it offended to a most dangerous degree by my absence."[1] He asked for their prayers.

"How disappointing! I have always wanted to hear the famous Augustine!" said Melania to her husband.

"His learned writings have meant so much to me and to all people of the empire," answered Pinianus. "If Augustine cannot come to Thagaste, I would like to visit Hippo Regius."

"Let us go as soon as it can be arranged," agreed Albina. "I am sure it will be an experience we will never forget."

"Pinianus! Pinianus! PINIANUS!"

The basilica of Hippo shook with the shouts of Augustine's congregation. Faces contorted, voices screamed, as the mob pushed the terrified, white-faced man toward the apse of the church.

"I refuse to ordain Pinianus as a priest!" yelled Augustine. The group of Hippo's elders who had gathered at the front of the basilica strained to hear him. "I will NOT!" shouted Augustine at the top of his lungs. "I will not force Pinianus to be a priest against his will. I have promised him, and I will not go back on my word. If you endeavor to compel me to break it, I will not be your bishop!" Augustine turned, walked back to his cathedra, and sat down.

"Perhaps another bishop will ordain him for us!" shouted

one man from the congregation. A volley of ayes followed.

"You cannot without my permission!" Augustine shouted back.

"It is because of that foul Alypius, who wants to keep his rich patron in Thagaste!" bellowed another.

"Yes, yes, it is because of Alypius!" the horde, crazed with rage, began to howl anew: "Down with Alypius! Down with the greedy liar! We want Pinianus!"

Alypius, who had left the bishops' bench when the shouting began, waved his arms angrily as he argued with the mob. Augustine could not hear a thing he said. The uproar increased as Pinianus left the building. An elder approached Augustine. "Pinianus says that if they ordain him against his will, he will leave Africa," he said.

Augustine closed his tired eyes. *I did not expect this sort of immigrant problem.* Augustine gestured to the elders, who withdrew to a slightly less noisy area of the church. The group argued and wrangled; a messenger from Pinianus stated he finally agreed to stay in Hippo if no one compelled him to be a priest.

"Silence! SILENCE!" Augustine roared. *My throat already hurts from preaching for three hours; I will not be able to speak for a week after this fiasco,* he thought. But the people finally quieted, and Augustine made the announcement.

To his surprise, a rumble of discussion followed his words. *If they wanted only his money, surely such a concession would suffice.*

"If you please, Your Holiness," said an elder, "the people want to know if Pinianus will agree to a promise that, should he ever become a priest, he will do so only in Hippo?"

A messenger from Pinianus once more confirmed the oath. An explosion of joy greeted this announcement—

until the deacon read an additional clause that defined the terms of Pinianus's leaving Hippo, such as invasion by barbarians or the state of his wife's health. An angry murmur rose, then a wave of rage swept the church.

"Lies! Treachery!" screamed the people.

Augustine exited out a back door to an area where Pinianus had taken refuge. "They believe you intentionally deceive them," said the bishop wearily.

"I do not!" said Pinianus indignantly. "I will speak with them," he said, "but not unless you go with me." Augustine nodded reluctantly; Pinianus took Augustine's arm and steered him back toward the doorway.

"People of Hippo!" Pinianus shouted. "I in no wise wish to deceive you; I keep my promises! If the clause regarding the extreme possibilities of my leaving disturbs you, I will strike it from the oath."

A tremendous roar greeted his words. This time, the congregation, a little worn with the day's events, began to disperse almost immediately, except for a few who continued their passionate argument with Alypius.

Pinianus was joined by his wife and mother-in-law, who had been seated with the women of the congregation. He and his wife turned quickly to leave, but his mother-in-law paused to give Augustine an icy glare. "Never in my life would I have expected such a tumult in your church," said Albina, her white lips tight with fear and anger. "They would have killed Pinianus if he had not made some concession to them."

The next day Pinianus left Hippo before dawn. "He is bound to Hippo as you and I are," Augustine explained to the bewildered townspeople. "We live here, but we come and go as we please. Surely, Pinianus also conducts his life freely, as we do."

Augustine dragged himself back to the bishop's house to write a long, apologetic letter to Albina and her children. *Somehow I doubt they will be moved to make a large contribution to Hippo for a while.*

Christian refugees, poor and wealthy, sought sanctuary in North Africa after the fall of Rome. But many pagans also left Italy to take refuge in Carthage, Hippo, and other cities in Numidia. They blamed Rome's fall on Christianity. If only Rome had remained true to its traditional gods, they said, she would have prospered. Augustine enjoyed the new friendships he made with these educated, honorable men who clung to Rome's past with the romantic desperation of those with little hope for the future. For twenty years Augustine had spent most of his time with everyday people; he cherished this opportunity to interact with men who possessed considerable knowledge of the classics and pondered deep philosophical questions.

But they cannot see their patriotism and their religious views are shaped by their despair, Augustine thought. He re-read the letter Marcellinus had sent. "It is important that all these difficulties [raised by pagans] be met by a full, thorough, and luminous reply (since the welcome answer of Your Holiness will doubtless be put into many hands). . . . I, therefore, not unmindful of your promise, but insisting on its [fulfillment], beseech you to write, on the questions submitted, treatises which will be of incredible service to the church, especially at the present time."[2]

Augustine sighed. He welcomed the opportunity to share his faith with such needy men; but at fifty-nine, he no longer possessed the energy of his youth. His schedule, already crammed with obligations, did not lend itself to writing a major treatise right now.

I had hoped my letters to Marcellinus would suffice to answer his friends' questions. Evidently, they only whet their appetites to ask more! But Augustine remembered his own days in Rome and Milan. *How I hungered for You, O my God! I forgot to eat and sleep as I searched for You in an endless desert, yet knew not it was You for which I yearned. Then Ambrose began to pour the cool, refreshing water of Your truth down my parched throat. . . .*

Now these men need a complete, documented answer. Will I deny it to them?

Augustine sat down and began to write *De civitate Dei (The City of God)*. In this enormous treatise, which numbered twenty-two books by the time he had finished in 426, Augustine exhibited his wide knowledge of classical history and philosophers.

First, Augustine carefully dissected Roman mythology, pouncing on its inconsistencies. He also insisted early Rome had not exhibited the fictional nobility attributed to it by contemporary pagans. In reality, Augustine said, it had portrayed excessive internal corruption, treachery, and violence. He questioned Rome's greedy expansionism as a pirate taken prisoner by Alexander the Great questioned his captor: "When that king had asked the man what he meant by keeping hostile possession of the sea, he answered with bold pride, 'What thou meanest by seizing the whole earth; but because I do it with a petty ship, I am called a robber, whilst thou who dost it with a great fleet art styled emperor.' "[3]

"How can these pagans believe that Rome fell because its leaders turned to Christ?" Augustine asked. In *The City of God* he cited past examples of other empires that met their end well before Christianity began: "The name of Christ had not yet been proclaimed in those parts of the earth when these kingdoms were lost and transferred through great destructions in war. For if, after more than twelve hundred years, when the kingdom was taken away from the Assyrians, the Christian religion had there already preached another eternal kingdom. . .what else would the foolish men of that nation have said, but that the kingdom which had been so long preserved, could be lost for no other cause than the desertion of their own religions and the reception of Christianity?"[4]

If I cite the history and fall of Rome to shake the pagans from their blind assumptions, perhaps they will release their grip on dead hopes and grasp the truth of the gospel, thought Augustine. *If they can understand the difference between earthly cities and the heavenly city, they will find the Wisdom for which many of the ancients yearned.*

"We must pray for Marcellinus!" cried Augustine in horror to his monks. "I have received word that he has been arrested by the authorities in Carthage as a corrupt, unchaste official. What utter nonsense! What idiocy! He had nothing to do with Heraclian."

Although the Catholics now officially held political and religious power in North Africa, such domination did not ensure their peaceful existence. News of barbarian advances in Europe assailed them with the arrival of every ship in Hippo's harbor. Numidia itself did not guarantee a safe haven from violence, as imperial troops struggled to put down Donatist uprisings and other political upheavals. Heraclian, the count of Africa, had engineered a rebellion and was promptly defeated. The imperial government now rounded up all of his alleged friends and allies.

"They accuse Marcellinus of unchaste behavior! I would laugh if this were not so frightening!" said Augustine. He and Marcellinus had written often since the Donatist

Collatio; the more Augustine corresponded with him, the more impressed he was with the layman's devotion to Christ and purity of heart. "I must do everything in my power to free him," said Augustine. As a bishop, he had rescued prisoners before. He knew the best ways to use his influence to help Marcellinus.

Augustine immediately sent a representative to Ravenna to plead Marcellinus's case before the royal court. Perhaps imperial authorities could override the actions of the Carthaginian officials, although Augustine recognized that during these turbulent times, imperial control of the provinces was imperfect at best. He contacted every person he knew who might be able to influence the local governor to let Marcellinus go. He visited his friend often and interceded on his behalf with the jailers so he would receive humane treatment.

When messengers brought word that Marcellinus had received a speedy trial just before the feast of Saint Cyprian in 413, Augustine did not doubt he would soon hear good news, as pardons were traditionally granted on that saint's feast day.

"Your Holiness! Marcellinus has been executed— beheaded!"

"What?" Augustine stared at his secretary stupidly. "What did you say?" *Surely I did not hear right; I am growing older. I did not hear right.*

The man's gaunt, white face floated before him like those of the demons in Augustine's childhood nightmares. "Marcellinus is dead, Your Holiness."

What is this world coming to? Nothing makes sense anymore, nothing. Marcellinus? Unchaste? Corrupt? Beheaded by the very people he served?

I do not want to live in this world any longer, Lord.

I want to live in Your city, the heavenly city where such atrocities do not exist. . . .

"Why art thou alarmed, because the kingdoms of the earth are perishing? Therefore hath a heavenly kingdom been promised thee, that thou mightest not perish with the kingdoms of the earth. . . . Thy Lord for whom thou art waiting, hath told thee, 'Nation shall rise up against nation, and kingdom against kingdom,' " preached Augustine.[5]

The fall of Rome had not sent mere ripples throughout the empire; it swept Romans everywhere with violent rapids of doubt and fear. Augustine's congregation listened to their bishop as if their breath depended on his next words. Despite the increasing turbulence of past decades, most of them had taken for granted that the empire, protected by God's hand, would last forever. Now the North Africans daily talked with refugees from Italy who had witnessed the unearthly screams of the conquering Visigoths, the murder of friends and relatives, the rape of maidens, the hungry flames devouring the city that represented the empire's eternal power, prestige, and culture. On Sundays the poor and rich, Italian and North African, all stood together in church, clinging to their faith and to each other as they heard Augustine preach about the heavenly kingdom.

"Why place we our hearts in the earth, when we see that the earth is being turned upside down?[6] He will come of whom it is said, 'and of His kingdom there shall be no end.' They who have promised this to earthly kingdoms have not been guided by truth, but have lied through flattery. A certain poet of theirs has introduced Jupiter speaking, and he says of the Romans:

'To them no bounds of empire I assign,

169

Nor term of years to their immortal line.'

"Most certainly truth makes no such answer. . . . Those things shall pass away which God hath Himself made; how much more rapidly shall that pass away which Romulus founded!"[7]

As I speak to the people, I speak all the more to myself, thought Augustine as he enjoyed his tranquil garden that Sunday evening. He, too, had seen the Roman Empire as God's chosen instrument to Christianize the world. The downfall of Rome had devastated him as well as his people. Augustine himself struggled with the continual unrest in Numidia, where unscrupulous politicians had executed Marcellinus. Even before those disastrous events, he found himself increasingly placing his focus on the world to come.

Dear Marcellinus, Augustine thought, *In the first five books of* The City of God, *I tried to answer the questions of your pagan friends. I will continue to do that as I write the series. But soon I will address the subject of supreme importance to all seekers of truth: the city of God, the heavenly city. The light of it overwhelms our earthly cities, which cannot last forever. Our citizenship here pales beside our eternal citizenship in the New Jerusalem.*

Augustine smiled sadly as he contemplated the glory of the setting sun over the mountains. *I imagine, Marcellinus, that you know far more about that than I do.*

In the last twelve books of *The City of God,* Augustine viewed human history, secular as well as biblical, as portraying two allegorical cities: Jerusalem, where loyal angels and redeemed humans served God, and Babylon, home of the devil, his demons, and the people who served them. "Though there are very many and great nations all over the earth, whose rites and customs, speech, arms, and dress, are distinguished by marked differences, yet there are no more than two kinds of human society, which we may justly call two cities, according to the language of our Scriptures. The one consists of those who wish to live after the flesh, the other of those who wish to live after the spirit.[8] Accordingly, two cities have been formed by two loves: the earthly by the love of self, even to the contempt of God; the heavenly by the love of God, even to the contempt of self."[9] Cain belonged to one kind of city, Abel the other, Augustine said; he also compared the two cities to Romulus and Remus, the twin founders of Rome.

Like the weeds and the wheat in Jesus' parable, the populaces of the two cities grew together. But Jesus Christ would separate them at the Last Judgment, Augustine declared. Jerusalem's inhabitants would stand on Christ's right, and Babylon's on His left. But while living on earth, the citizens of the heavenly Jerusalem would no doubt feel like strangers in a foreign land, as the Israelites had while dwelling in Babylon.

"My family has lived in Carthage for more than two centuries," said Augustine's friend Tacitus, a nobleman with whom he enjoyed many deep discussions. "We have been Christians for nearly that long. Yet it is only in the last few years that I feel as if I do not belong here." He stared at Augustine in bewilderment.

"Why is that?" asked Augustine.

Tacitus shrugged. "My pagan friends blame Christians for the fall of Rome; whereas we used to enjoy our debates, I now sense open hostility toward my point of view. If only we Christians return to the true Roman way of life, they say, all will be well."

"In other words, if we bow down to senseless idols, celebrate the wanton Saturnalia, and watch bloody circus games and lecherous theatrical productions, Rome will return to its former glory?"

Tacitus grinned. "Would you care to attend our next debate?"

"With pleasure," said Augustine.

If only Christians understood our true citizenship exists not on earth, but in the heavenly city, thought Augustine. He preached about the New Jerusalem at every opportunity.

He also tried to help his people deal with their sufferings and uncertain earthly future. The difficult days would generate maturity and fortitude in their lives, Augustine told his congregation. God's discipline would produce positive results, as the pressing of the olives grown on their hillsides produced abundant, useful oil. These were the last days, and what could they expect? "Wonderest thou that the world is failing? Wonder that the world is grown old. It is as a man who is born, and grows up, and waxes old. . . and is full of troubles. . . . Choose not then to cleave to this aged world, and to be unwilling to grow young in Christ, who telleth thee, 'The world is perishing, the world is waxing old, the world is failing; is distressed by the heavy breathing of old age. But do not fear, Thy youth shall be renewed as the eagle's.' "[10]

seventeen

B efore he died, Marcellinus told me to beware of Pelagius and his ideas," said Augustine to Alypius, who had come for a short visit. "He feared Pelagius's influence confused new converts. I have read some of Pelagius's work and found it provocative. The man writes with excellent content and style. Refreshing, when so many authors nowadays do neither! He obviously has pursued a superior education and seems a model of Christian piety. Perhaps Marcellinus was overreacting."

"Marcellinus never impressed me as a man who would make unsubstantiated judgments," said Alypius.

"True," said Augustine. "It would have been highly uncharacteristic of him. Perhaps it was a matter of semantics; he possibly misunderstood Pelagius."

"I doubt it," said Alypius. "I have heard much of Pelagius during my visits to Rome. He may have begun his career as a British provincial, but he has become one of the most influential laymen in Rome while we have kept our eyes on our own little corner of the world."

"If fighting Donatism had not absorbed most of our

energies, perhaps we could have paid more attention to the rest of the empire," said Augustine. "And if the Roman bishops had kept us informed of the terrible political and religious climate before Rome fell, we might also have become more involved."

He frowned, then brought his thoughts back to the subject at hand. "Is there reason to doubt the integrity of Pelagius?"

"His integrity is unquestioned. His North African disciple, Caelestius, also exhibits many admirable qualities, although he is a young hothead. Caelestius gave up his wealth and status to become one of the *servi Dei*. I did hear that he questions whether the human race inherited the sin of Adam. He even disputes the necessity of infant baptism."

"I know," said Augustine. "I heard as much and thought of him when I was writing *De peccatorum meritis et remissione et de baptismo parvulorum (On the Merits and Forgiveness of Sins and on Infant Baptism)* and *De spiritu et littera (On the Spirit and the Letter)*. But Aurelius and the authorities in Carthage did not immediately censure Caelestius, so I occupied myself with other important matters. Paulinus of Milan was the one who initiated the denial of his ordination in Carthage. But the eastern empire bishops ordained Caelestius in Ephesus."

"But no one has censured Pelagius," said Alypius. "Some say he places far too much emphasis on man's ability to perfect himself. He shows no patience whatsoever with those who do not wish to lead a life completely dedicated to Christ."

"I can sympathize with that." Sometimes Augustine tired of dealing with his rowdy, immature congregation. "Alypius, how do *you* see Pelagius?"

Alypius paused for some time. "I am not sure, Augustine. I have read some of his work, and I heard him speak once.

His true devotion to God and his natural genius in communicating his views impressed me. But Pelagius enjoys hearing himself, I believe, a little too much."

"I have *never* been guilty of that sin," chuckled Augustine.

"Of course, you haven't." Alypius grinned, but his eyes quickly lost their twinkle. "There is a cold fire in Pelagius that I distrust, Augustine."

"Or do we jealous old men distrust his talent, dynamism, and influence in high places? After all, Paulinus of Nola and Proba and her family give him their complete support." Augustine had met Proba when she and her family left Rome after that city's fall. The devout widow of the wealthiest man in the empire corresponded regularly with Augustine.

"I know my flesh dislikes his prominence," admitted Alypius. "For that I ask my Savior's pardon. Nevertheless, Augustine, I think Pelagius warrants closer scrutiny."

"I wish I had not been absent when he passed through Hippo on his way to Carthage," said Augustine. "I would understand Pelagius better if we had talked. And he would understand me."

And fear you, added Alypius silently. Augustine had never lost the charisma that attracted people of all ages and backgrounds. But the Donatist conflict had left its mark; the charming, gray-haired bishop could metamorphose into a raging warrior if Augustine detected heresy in a writer or speaker.

"I intend to pay more attention to the teachings of Pelagius and Caelestius," said Augustine. "I will also discuss the situation with Aurelius of Carthage and ask him to do the same. While I find no concrete reason to question Pelagius's scriptural accuracy so far, it is well to be vigilant."

"I hope Pelagius proves our suspicions wrong," said Alypius.

"So do I. Our blessed Lord knows we have enough concerns as it is."

"Be ye therefore perfect, even as your Father which is in heaven is perfect" (Matthew 5:48).

How can Pelagius use Jesus' own words to destroy His church? Augustine wondered. *But after dealing with the Donatists, why should this surprise me? And Satan himself used the Scriptures for his own ends.*

For Augustine was convinced that Pelagius did not speak the truth. He began to write furiously against what he considered a dire threat to Christians. He sent Orosius, an aggressive priest who shared his concerns, to Palestine, where Pelagius would meet with Jerome and other prominent bishops in December 415. Later, after procuring records of the conference, Augustine described the proceedings in his *De gestis pelagii* (On the Proceedings of Pelagius).

"Pelagius. . .wrote thus, 'A man is able, if he likes, to be without sin,' and 'He worthily raises his hands to God, and with a good conscience does he pour out his prayer, who is able to say, "Thou, O Lord, knowest how holy, and harmless, and pure from all injury and iniquity and violence, are the hands which I stretch out to Thee; how righteous, and pure, and free from all deceit, are the lips with which I offer to Thee my supplication, that Thou wouldst have mercy upon me." ' "[1]

"Does this sound similar to the Pharisee's prayer in the Gospels, Alypius?" Augustine raged. "Such self-congratulation dares stand before God?"

"No wonder the Spirit gave us no rest about the man!" agreed Alypius.

Augustine recorded more of the proceedings: "To all this Pelagius said in answer: 'We asserted that a man could be without sin, and could keep God's commandments if he wished; for this capacity has been given to him by God. . .if any person were converted from his sins, he could by his own labour and God's grace be without sin. . . . As for the other statements which they have made against us, they are not to be found in our books, nor have we at any time said such things.' "[2]

"How could the bishops swallow such nonsense?" Augustine snorted. "They did not examine his works! After that ridiculous conference, I gained access to some of Pelagius's writings through the generosity of some of my holy brothers. In them, Pelagius clearly makes the claims he denied before the bishops!"

Several other doctrinal stands attributed to Pelagius had also worried Augustine: "That infants, even if they die unbaptized, have eternal life. That rich men, even if they are baptized, unless they renounce all, have, whatever good they may seem to have done, nothing of it reckoned to them; neither can they possess the kingdom of God."[3] Augustine also suspected Pelagius did not believe in the doctrine of original sin.

"I once thought he was a student of Saint Paul!" said Augustine. He glared at Orosius, who had returned after the meeting in Jerusalem. "Has he ever in his *life* read Paul's epistle to the Romans?"

"Evidently not, your holiness," answered Orosius, who had not looked forward to this homecoming.

"How did the man manipulate fourteen bishops— including Jerome!—into seeing him as harmless?"

"First, he disavowed any connections with Caelestius or his views," said Orosius. "That seemed to give him credence in their eyes. Too, there were language difficulties. I speak no Greek. The two bishops from Gaul required translators.

Somehow, Pelagius convinced all that Jerome, you, and I were engaged in a vindictive war of petty semantics." He gave a helpless shrug. "Pelagius is a master at gathering support."

"How well I know," said Augustine grimly. Pelagius's "fan clubs" of organized, well-educated followers sent his writings all over the empire. They had circulated copies of his letter to Demetrias, the niece of Proba and one of the richest heiresses in the western world, who had decided to become a nun. Pelagius had taken this golden opportunity to emphasize his elite connections and to advocate his views on the perfecting of man and the renouncing of riches. His supporters had sent abroad many copies of his treatise *On Nature* which strongly reacted against Augustine's unyielding view of God as sovereign and man as helpless in his sin. "I know all about his superior abilities as a politician and propagandist," Augustine muttered. "But when unrighteous doctrines endanger Christians, Pelagius will find I *never* give in."

He stood up. "We have a busy day ahead of us, Orosius. I want you to talk with Aurelius. Tomorrow we will address the conference."

"What conference?" asked Orosius.

"Most of the three hundred North African bishops already have arrived in Carthage to discuss this situation," said Augustine. "The others will meet with Alypius and me in Milevis soon. Did you think I would waste a moment in the face of such an emergency?"

In a very short time, the North African bishops unanimously condemned Pelagius and sent an impressive collection of documents to Innocent, bishop of Rome: two detailed treatises against Pelagianism, a copy of Pelagius's *On Nature,* and a lengthy cover letter signed by Augustine, Aurelius, and Alypius. Another letter addressed to Pelagius insinuated the theologian had refused to carry on an open discussion with Augustine.

Did Innocent realize, the North Africans inquired, that Pelagius's declaration that man could perfect himself would undercut the hard-won authority and unity of the Catholic Church? These self-perfected saints would hardly listen to bishops. How then could the church remain effective in saving men's souls?

Certainly such destructive concepts should be censured! answered Innocent. But did they actually permeate current thought? He would investigate. He would command Pelagius and Caelestius to come to Rome and define and defend their points of view.

The North African church hierarchy breathed a sigh of relief. So far, so good. But Innocent died in March 417 before the meeting, and Zosimus, a bishop who always took the easiest path available, inherited his position. He quizzed Caelestius, but not too thoroughly, as Caelestius's charismatic and powerful personality dazzled him. Zosimus decided Caelestius had crossed no important theological lines. He then invited Pelagius to his court, and was so impressed by the man's faith that he afterward rebuked Augustine and all the North Africans who would vilify such a man. The piety of Pelagius had moved them all to tears, he said. Although Augustine was a brilliant man, Zosimus declared, he had resorted to nitpicking in the name of religion.

Augustine launched a furious writing campaign while the North Africans waited for the tide to turn. He flooded the Roman Empire with pamphlets against the Pelagians. He wrote a lengthy, vehement letter to Paulinus of Nola. He tried to gain the support of Dardanus, a former prefect of Gaul, a pious Christian with enormous wealth and influence in the far western empire. He pleaded with Lady Juliana, a rich Italian aristocrat and the mother of Demetrias, to "avoid

179

opinions opposed to the grace of God," and "not to lend an ear to those men who, by their mischievous writings, often corrupt our holy faith."[4] His entreaty did not impress Juliana. She and her devout family identified heresy with the denial of the trinity, as believed by the Arians. Juliana, as well as Proba and many of the noble Christian families, considered Augustine a picky provincial clergyman with a narrow-minded ax to grind, with his emphasis on grace and free will.

"Intolerant? I, intolerant?" asked Augustine indignantly. "Pelagius, like the Donatists, seeks to restrict the grace of God to a minuscule elite who perfectly keep the laws of God—as defined by Pelagius, of course! Only *they* deserve His grace! God would accept only monks and nuns as true Christians! He has no heart for the weak and wandering sheep that Christ Himself seeks! And he would relegate all rich Christians to hell!" Augustine threw *On Nature* at the wall in frustration. "I would burn this detestable treatise," he shouted, "except that I need it to refute that man! And refute him, I will!"

Another aged theologian applauded Augustine's efforts against Pelagius; he, too, launched his own campaign against Pelagius's theology and fought him as vehemently as Augustine. Battling heresy had brought Jerome and Augustine together as nothing else had. "You have, with the ardour of unshaken faith, stood your ground against opposing storms," Augustine wrote, "and preferred, so far as this was in your power, to be delivered from Sodom. . . . Go on and prosper! You are renowned throughout the whole world; Catholics revere and look up to you as the restorer of the ancient faith, and—which is a token of yet more illustrious glory—all heretics abhor you. They persecute me also with equal hatred."[5]

Pelagius did not wish to leave the church; he and his followers hoped to reform the church and purge it of the widespread mediocrity evidenced in the lifestyles of many Christians. He charged that Augustine's passivity in the face of evil and his emphasis on the flesh versus the spirit echoed unpleasantly of Manichaeanism. But he extended the olive branch to Augustine through Albina, Pinianus, and Melania, their bewildered mutual friends. Pelagius strongly condemned "the man who either thinks or says that the grace of God, whereby 'Christ Jesus came into the world to save sinners,' is not necessary not only for every hour and for every moment, but also for every act of our lives: and those who endeavour to disannul it deserve everlasting punishment."[6]

Pinianus delivered the message, then asked Augustine to accept Pelagius as a brother in Christ.

But Augustine answered with a two-volume treatise, *De gratia Christi et de peccato originali (A Treatise on the Grace of Christ and Original Sin)*, in which he asserted Pelagius was, in fact, a theological wolf in sheep's clothing. "Now, whoever hears these words, and is ignorant of the opinion which [Pelagius] has clearly enough expressed in his books. . .would certainly suppose that the views he holds are in strict accordance with the truth. But whoever notices what he openly declares in them, cannot fail to regard these statements with suspicion."[7] Pelagius agreed that God's grace redeemed man and taught him God's laws, said Augustine. But Pelagius also believed that once converted, a man could achieve perfection by his own efforts. Heresy, said Augustine. Pure and simple.

While Augustine fought a relentless battle against Pelagius, he wrote other works: *Contra sermonem Arianorum (Against an Arian Sermon)* and several books of *The City of God*. He waited. And waited.

"How long wilt thou forget me, O Lord? for ever? how

long wilt thou hide thy face from me?" (Psalm 13:1) prayed Augustine in his garden late one night when sleep eluded him. *No one believes in God's sovereignty more than I do, but each day brings more defeats than victories. Sometimes I can hardly drag my aching old bones out of bed in the morning. The Pelagians claim to have won. Perhaps they have. Ambrose defied an army outside his church. Will soldiers march on my basilica too?* Sometimes Augustine could almost hear the echo of heavy feet and the clash of swords as he served before the altar. *Will they throw me into prison? Will the Pelagians drag me before the Roman courts to suffer humiliation and exile?*

Without warning, riots erupted in Jerusalem, fueled, it seemed, by the Pelagians. Then sudden uprisings took place in Rome, where Pelagian followers attacked a prominent retired administrator. No one knew the origin or motivation of the angry mobs that terrorized both cities. Pelagians and Augustinians pointed accusing fingers at each other. But Emperor Honorius determined that Pelagius and Caelestius were to blame. He sentenced them to immediate exile and directed authorities to prosecute any supporters of their doctrines. Despite his earlier support of the two, Zosimus, Rome's bishop, quickly concurred and censured them. After the other Italian bishops signed his condemnation, Pelagianism would be officially banished from the empire.

Augustine and his followers celebrated the sudden victory!

But the battle had not ended. Zosimus died in 418, and Pelagius's followers attacked his ruling. Led by the eminent young bishop, Julian of Eclanum, a number of Italian bishops appealed to the imperial court. They insisted Pelagianism upheld the intrinsic excellence of God's creation and the nobility of man, His creature. God in the Scriptures had granted man free will, they declared; surely the court could not sanction Augustine's ridiculous and oppressive doctrines of predestination.

But Augustine's uncanny ability to know the right people at the right time paid off; Valerius, a devout Catholic and court general with a fervent dislike of infidels, frustrated the Pelagians' efforts to bring their case before the court in Ravenna. He also maneuvered the enforcement of laws against bishops with Pelagian sympathies. His cavalry officers, loyal to their commander, readily carried out Valerius's convictions, especially as they had been promised a gift of eighty beautiful Numidian horses by Alypius, who carried on most of the negotiations between North Africa and Rome with his usual court savvy.

The Italians could not believe it. How could a man of God coerce them into accepting his beliefs by political power and military force, rather than intellectual and spiritual superiority? But to Augustine, the Pelagian creed that man could and must perfect himself constituted a danger that threatened all Christians. He had to do everything in his power to correct such a fatal error. When Augustine spoke of reaching out to his enemy, the Pelagian, he said, "We do not sincerely love him unless we wish him to be good, which he cannot be until he be delivered from the sin of cherished enmities."[8] He told the bishop Sixtus, who had foresworn his earlier allegiance to Pelagius, that he had an obligation to see "that those be punished with wholesome severity who dare to prate more openly their declaration of that error, most dangerously hostile to the Christian name [i.e. Pelagianism]. . . ."[9]

Although Pelagius, Caelestius, and Julian were exiled, Pelagianism did not die. Neither did Augustine's efforts to defeat it. *I will not keep silent. As long as God grants me breath, parchment, and pen, I will fight for His cause.*

eighteen

W here do you come from, child?" Augustine asked gently.

The terrified young girl shrank as if he had struck her. She covered her face with hands that fluttered like a moth's wings. The chains that hung from her wrists gave a raucous rattle. Augustine longed to reassure her but feared he would only frighten her more.

A bear-like slave trader emerged from the tavern doorway to strike down the fragile, black-robed old man who dared interfere with his property. Augustine might have been near his seventieth birthday, but his steely gaze bolted the man to the wall. If one injured a bishop, the slave trader knew, God might strike him dead! Muttering, he slunk back into the inn to buy another drink.

"He is gone," said Augustine. "You may speak freely with me now."

"She knows he will beat us when he returns," said a teenaged boy whose manacled wrists, like the girl's, were attached to a post outside the tavern. He spoke in broken Latin, his voice flat, emotionless.

"Perhaps I can be of help."

The boy said nothing. Augustine could not repress a shiver as he tried to look him in the face. Augustine expected to find raw anger or smoldering cynicism in his eyes. They stared back at him, blank as a statue's.

But the girl spoke, hesitantly at first, then eagerly in Punic, her thin, bruised face alive, urgent.

I can understand only a few words here and there! thought Augustine in frustration. The girl tugged insistently on the boy's ragged sleeve. He gave a slight shrug, then interpreted. They came from a farm near Vegesela. A week ago, as she and her mother were working in their garden, strangers in foreign clothes had swept down from the hills on powerful horses, wailing like demons. One had grabbed her, laughing as he threw her across his saddle. Another had ripped her baby brother from her mother's back and slammed his fist in her face when she screamed and clawed at his eyes. The strangers set their house on fire, howling with glee when it collapsed in the flames.

The young girl's voice rose, fell, wept, whispered. The boy recited. When Augustine asked him to recall his own experiences that terrible day, he answered that he, his father, and his older brother had been harvesting their barley when the riders appeared. They killed the others and took him captive. He did not know why they spared him. They took all the grain too.

"Were they barbarians from the south? The west?" Vandals had already conquered most of Spain. Any day Augustine expected to hear they had landed on the shores of North Africa.

"Not south," answered the boy. "And I have never heard the language from the far west."

"Did they speak Latin?"

185

He nodded. "Some spoke like you; others had accents I have heard along the docks in Hippo."

The slave trader appeared once more. "They need food and water," said Augustine. He sat down beside the young slaves. The man grunted, but he bought two large pieces of hot bread from a vendor and filled two dirty cups from a jug on his horse. Augustine remained until the teens had wolfed down every bite.

"If you will hand me that jug, I will pour another cup of water for each," said Augustine. The slave trader growled, and his eyes flashed with a dangerous gleam. "What sort of profit will you make," asked Augustine coldly, "if you abuse your wares? You would not mistreat a good horse or ox. Besides," he added firmly, "you have a Master in heaven, and He will require their blood at your hand."

The slave trader wore a wicked-looking knife at his belt, but he quailed before the elderly bishop. "Take heart," said Augustine to the children. "God is the Friend of the friendless, the Defender of orphans. He will not forget you." Before he turned to leave, he saw a tiny spark of gratitude in the boy's dead eyes.

"They do nothing about it, Alypius!" Augustine exploded. "Captains anchor their slave ships in the harbor in broad daylight! Long lines of slaves are goaded aboard like cattle. And no official in all Hippo sees a thing!"

"No doubt they are paid well for their blindness," said Alypius.

"No doubt," said Augustine, wincing. *I dreamed of that slave child last night and the night before. Has that bully abused her since we parted? Has she had anything to eat?* He tried to shake the image from his mind. "I knew before the boy told me the murderers were not desert nomads. I'm sure some were local thugs who help supply Europe with healthy North African workers! The barbarians have wreaked havoc on farms in Italy and Gaul; large landowners need many slaves to get back on their feet. How convenient to forget the 'slaves' they buy and sell so cheaply are, in fact, full citizens of the empire!"

"So far Hippo Christians have paid ransom for 120 captives," said Alypius.

"At least a few of these unfortunate people will not be worked to death in the fields or sold as prostitutes," said Augustine. Once more the slave girl's intense young face haunted his thoughts.

"The lawsuit brought against us by the harbor authorities remains stalled in court," said Alypius.

"So for now they are frustrated in their evil actions. How sad that the godless persecute clergy when they reach out to the helpless," said Augustine.

Alypius nodded grimly. "I cannot be optimistic at this point. I know no relevant laws to wield against them."

"Then find some, Alypius," said Augustine. "You are far more versed in imperial law than I am. You will find the right laws; then I will present the written case to Rome."

Alypius nodded, his face as resolute as his friend's. An unexpected grin showed through his sparse gray beard. "How can anyone resist our combined genius?" he asked.

"The kidnappers and the slave traders," said Augustine, "have no chance."

Augustine turned his weary steps towards the bishop's house. Much as he enjoyed the young monks' company, tonight he needed quiet. *So much to do,* he thought. *The workload of a servant of God does not lighten just because he passes seventy years. If anything, the burden grows heavier.*

For one thing, Emperor Honorius might have exiled and humiliated Julian of Eclanum, but he could not stop Julian's fierce battle against Augustine. Julian had fled to the eastern empire, where the church often welcomed his views. From a safe distance, he blasted Augustine with his well-written, persuasive treatises against original sin and the injustice of predestination. As a well-educated, aristocratic young Pelagian, Julian lauded man and his ability to perfect himself, and he possessed the skills to perpetuate his ideas in the western empire, as well. Augustine would soon discover he had met his prolific match.

Augustine had written the *Enchiridion ad Laurentium de fide spe et caritate (A Handbook on Faith, Hope, and Love)* as a doctrinal guidebook to help dispel Pelagian influences. He also wrote *De Nuptiis et concupiscentia (On Marriage and Concupiscence),* to answer the questions of Valerius, the imperial commander who had helped secure the exile of Pelagius. Augustine was a Manichaean in disguise, said Valerius's Pelagian friends. According to them, Augustine believed sexuality was physical and therefore evil just as the Manichaeans did. Augustine tried to dissipate this confusion by affirming the validity of marriage. But he also said that sexual desire, even within marriage, was a product of Adam's original sin and that babies, although created within the scriptural context of marriage, were depraved because they inherited that original sin.

Julian, whose simple, Eden-like marriage ceremony had been blessed by none other than Paulinus of Nola, wrote an immediate, scathing answer to Augustine's theology—four volumes. Augustine responded by adding another volume to *On Marriage and Concupiscence,* plus a six-volume new series he entitled *Contra Julianum (Against Julian).*

Now Julian has written eight more books in his attempt

to undermine the truths of God! thought Augustine. *That obnoxious young fool tries my sense of charity more than any man I have encountered.* Augustine, determined to defeat his adversary, had already begun his enormous work, *Contra Julianum opus imperfectum (Against Julian, an Unfinished Book),* over which he would labor until his death.

One of the most frustrating aspects of this conflict is that Julian possesses plenty of leisure time to conduct his little war against me, thought Augustine. *Wealthy patrons support him in a stable, prosperous part of the empire, while I serve a frightened people threatened by the Vandals.*

Other concerns pulled at Augustine's weary mind. He maintained a correspondence with some monasteries and nunneries and often found himself dealing with theological tangles and practical concerns. Augustine's stand on predestination had inflamed rebellion in some monastic circles. "Why give up the joys of a wife and family if God chooses His elect with no regard to a man's faith or devotion?" asked monks in Hadrumetum, one of North Africa's chief monasteries. "Why live an ascetic life away loved ones if God does not reward such devotion with His presence?" A number of them refused to work in the fields. Others defied their leaders' correction: "If God controls all things, then the abbot need not rebuke us. God will change us," said the rebels. Monks elsewhere claimed they could mystically comprehend the Scriptures without study or education.

"What nonsense!" said Augustine. "What idiocy!" He began a collection of Scripture that defined stringent standards of right and wrong behavior.

Augustine settled ongoing clerical squabbles, including those of disgruntled nuns at the abbey where his sister, Perpetua, had presided before her death. He commanded they obey their prioress, pool their financial resources without comparison or complaint, and concern themselves more with spiritual matters than material: They must not quibble about insignificant things, such as clothing, said Augustine. How could they all complain so bitterly about their ugly dresses? "Judge how far deficient you must be in the inner holy dress of the heart, when you quarrel with each other about the clothing of the body."[1] Don't be obsessed by the cleanliness of your body or clothes, Augustine advised, "lest the indulgence of undue solicitude about spotless raiment produce inward stains upon your souls. Let the washing of the body and the use of baths be not constant, but at the usual interval assigned to it, i.e. once in a month."[2]

I suppose their problems should not surprise me. But such things seem so trivial in the face of eternity. Augustine chuckled at the thought of the gorgeous embroidered silk robe a grateful correspondent had sent him. How could a grizzled old graybeard with skinny legs and ankles do justice to its beauty? For the sake of friendship, he would keep the gift; but upon his death, it would be sold immediately and the proceeds given to the poor.

I do my best, Holy Lord, Augustine thought. *But sometimes I make mistakes. Certainly I did in my appointment of Antoninus of Fussala.* Augustine had chosen the young man as bishop of a small town fifty miles from Hippo, hoping he would serve the people well because he spoke Punic fluently. But soon horrendous rumors reached his ears. Augustine, who hated travel even more as an elderly man, made the rugged journey to Fussala to investigate. Antoninus had exploited and abused his people; he'd even stolen stones from their homes to build his beautiful bishop's palace! Augustine confronted Antoninus, who defied him. Augustine knew he would have to arrange for the younger man's removal through higher channels when he returned to Hippo.

Thanks be to God such a disaster rarely occurred in my appointments, Augustine thought. But he paid dearly for his miscalculations in the case of Antoninus.

Angry and resentful, the people blamed Augustine; as they spoke only Punic, he found it impossible to explain or apologize. One Sunday morning, the entire church, including the nuns, had turned their backs and left when he began his homily. Worst of all, for weeks Augustine could find no one to guide him and his party back to Hippo. He remained in the miserable, hostile little town until rescued by a sympathetic trader who spoke Latin. Once back in Hippo, Augustine immediately began proceedings to remove the selfish, arrogant young bishop. But Antoninus appealed to powerful Italian authorities to protect him. Augustine found himself once more embroiled in a bitter dispute. *Thank You, Lord, that Celestine, the new bishop of Rome, listened to me.* He hoped he never had to deal with such a situation again.

At least I do not have to referee the everyday lawsuits. I have spent untold years haggling over the inheritance of land and farm animals! thought Augustine. He had officially handed over his bishopric to Eraclius a few years before during mass one warm September morning in 426. The people packed the Hippo Church of Peace, with many standing at the doors and windows.

"I know that churches are wont to be disturbed after the decease of their bishops by ambitious or contentious parties, and I feel it to be my duty to take measures to prevent this community from suffering. . . . I wish to have for my successor the presbyter Eraclius."

"To God be thanks! To Christ be praise!" chanted the congregation twenty-three times. "O Christ, hear us; may Augustin[e] live long!" they shouted sixteen times, and "We

191

will have thee as our father, thee as our bishop!" eight times.

"May He who has sent him to me preserve him! Preserve him safe, preserve him blameless, that as he gives me joy while I live, he may fill my place when I die," said Augustine.

"To God be thanks! To Christ be praise!" chorused the people thirty-six times, and "O Christ, hear us; may Augustine live long!" thirteen times.[3] They continued their loud acclamations throughout Augustine's speech.

His old eyes had brimmed with tears, but their faces remained clear in his mind. Most of his parishioners could not remember when he had not been bishop of Hippo. He had baptized them as wriggling, screaming newborn babies, and lately he had baptized their grandchildren. Many had infuriated him with their love for astrology, bizarre miracles, and pagan celebrations. Their continual indifference to spiritual concerns frustrated him. But their passionate loyalty had delighted him down through the years. He loved them. With everything in him, he had loved and served them, and he believed the naming of his successor to be one more important act of service.

"We all are mortal, and the day which shall be the last of life on earth is to every man at all times uncertain," Augustine had preached that morning.[4]

Three years later, he still found it difficult to believe he had been a priest for almost forty years—and that his ministry's end loomed. *I am learning to hand the reins over to Eraclius, but it has not been easy.*

Augustine spent much of his newfound leisure studying the Bible. How he had dreamed of spending his days pondering the magnificent, mystical, yet infinitely practical truths of the Scriptures! Now he could do so uninterrupted by petty problems.

He also began the tedious work of cataloging his

extensive personal library. *The truths God has given me to share must not die with me.* He carefully reviewed all his works and corrected them in a volume called *Retractationes (Reconsiderations).*

While Augustine cherished the serene hours spent in study, contemplation, and writing, he knew they were numbered. Too soon, reports of the arrival of Vandal soldiers on the far west coast of Africa reached a terrified Regius Hippo.

They are coming, thought Augustine. *The Vandals are coming, and only God can stop them.*

nineteen

Neither we nor the angels can understand, as God understands, the peace which God Himself enjoys."[1] *I speak of peace on this Sabbath morning,* thought Augustine as he preached. And the murderous Vandals advance daily toward our city.

His congregation, rich and poor, stood together in uncharacteristic silence. Their hollow eyes pleaded for hope.

" 'Now we see through a glass, darkly; but then face to face.' This vision is reserved as the reward of our faith; and of it the Apostle John also says, 'When He shall appear, we shall be like Him, for we shall see Him as He is.' "[2]

Genseric, the clever, resourceful Vandal king, stopped at nothing to gain wealth. Many in his army of eighty thousand men followed the Arian creed; they believed the warlike God of the Old Testament supported their cause. Genseric and his Vandals swept through Mauretania with little resistance and now menaced Numidia.

Augustine had commanded his bishops to remain with their flocks in the face of the onslaught. But he had received a number of panicked letters from clergymen in surrounding towns, among them Honoratus: "I do not see what good we can do to ourselves or to the people by continuing to remain in the churches, except to see before our eyes men slain, women outraged, churches burned, ourselves expiring amid torments applied in order to extort from us what we do not possess."[3] Augustine did not think the man's concerns were exaggerated. Already he had received word of the killings by torture of two bishops.

But Augustine continued to speak to his congregation of life in Paradise. "For in that life necessity shall have no place, but full, certain, secure, everlasting felicity."[4]

When the Vandals sacked Calama, Possidius fled to Hippo. "It was like Judgment Day, Augustine," he said when he could speak. "The fires of hell could not burn more fiercely than those the Vandals set. They ravished the women, even the nuns. . . ."

Augustine pitied the young, with their short lives in jeopardy. As a tired old man, he, too, feared the hunger, the fires, and his own murder, which, he knew, would be a slow and painful one. But Augustine had braved many storms through the years. He would trust the One he called his "True Life" and his "Steadfast Sweetness," who would guide him to that city of which he now spoke.[5]

What a Paradise! Even though Augustine shook with illness and old age, his voice rang with power as he preached. "[God] shall be the end of our desires who shall be seen without end. . .praised without weariness. . . . In that city, then, there shall be free will, one in all the citizens, and indivisible in each, delivered from all ill, filled with all good, enjoying indefeasibly the delights of eternal joys, oblivious of sins, oblivious of sufferings, and yet not so oblivious of its deliverance as to be ungrateful to its Deliverer."[6]

How I long for that City, oh Lord.

"Paste them there," said Augustine, pointing with a feeble hand.

His faithful assistant Linus, himself now gray-haired, placed the copies of David's psalms above the old priest's bed. Augustine began to repeat the precious words of penitence to himself. Tears ran down his wrinkled face.

"Is there something I can do to ease your pain, Your Holiness?" asked Linus.

"Only pray for me, my son. My end draws near." A brief ghost of a twinkle appeared in his sunken eyes. "This fever may cheat the Vandals of an opportunity to kill me."

The Vandals had blockaded Hippo's harbor and laid siege for more than a year. Its emaciated inhabitants expected the enemy to burst through the city gates any day now.

"Your friends insist on seeing you, but I told them you were too ill," added Linus.

If only Alypius were here! But Augustine's closest friend had himself died two years before. "I appreciate their kindness," said Augustine, "but I wish to pray alone before I die. They may come when I take my meals and directly after the doctor visits; otherwise, I must have solitude."

"Yes, Your Holiness," said Linus.

Augustine turned to the wall once more and began intoning the psalms. For ten days he prayed. On August 28, A.D. 430, the seventy-six-year-old bishop died and was buried by his grieving congregation.

The Vandals attacked Hippo almost a year later, burning and plundering its contents as feared. Possidius escaped from the ravaged city, taking Augustine's last letter to the other bishops. Later, after the Vandals had moved farther east, he returned to the ruins of the city where Augustine had served.

How can Augustine's library possibly have survived this devastation? Everywhere Possidius looked, charred wreckage met his eyes. But Augustine's library, with its extensive collection of classics, his own ninety-three works, plus stacks of letters and sermons, had miraculously escaped the destruction. Possidius found them carefully preserved in their small cabinets, much as Augustine had left them.

There are thousands of pages here, thought Possidius. *Thousands and thousands! No man could read all this in one lifetime, let alone write it! Are any of his books missing?*

Possidius began a checklist. Leafing through them brought back many memories of the tender, brilliant old warrior who never shrunk from a theological battle. Later Possidius would write a biography of his mentor.

What a man Augustine was, marveled Possidius. *Sometimes I wonder if we will survive without his presence. We depended on him so. Every philosopher, priest, or student who knocked on his door with a question received an answer; every letter got a detailed response. And all because he delighted in his God.*

" 'Delight thyself in the Lord,' " Augustine had told his congregation, " 'and He shall give thee the desires of thy heart.' There is a pleasure of the heart to which that bread of heaven is sweet. . . . Give me a man that loves, and he feels what I say. Give me one that longs, one that hungers, one that is travelling in this wilderness, and thirsting and panting after the fountain of his eternal home; give such, and he knows what I say."[7]

Certainly you were such a man, Augustine, thought Possidius. Tears wet his cheeks; he shielded the books from the moisture with a careful hand. *You were a man in love with your God.*

Possidius grimaced as he wrestled with the massive *City*

197

of God; he remembered it had presented special problems to Augustine's bookbinder. His mentor's towering intellect awed Possidius, even after their friendship of many years. Augustine had challenged his world, both pagan and Christian elements, western and eastern. Down through the centuries, his doctrinal treatises would impact Roman Catholic, Protestant, and Eastern Orthodox Christianity. Thousands of priests and pastors would study Augustine's commentaries for spiritual guidance. Theological giants such as the Venerable Bede, Thomas Aquinas, Martin Luther, and John Calvin, as well as more modern scholars including Adolf von Harnack and Maurice Blondel, would weigh the works of Augustine as they, too, sought True Wisdom.

Possidius had always regarded Augustine's genius with deep respect. But scholarly achievements faded in importance as gentle memories of his mentor's everyday ministry now overwhelmed him: Augustine's care of sick parishioners, his steadfast kindness to the needy, his patience with young monks as he taught them in the monastery garden. *Why did he endure our ignorance? We must have driven him mad!* Possidius skimmed the last page of the heavy *City of God* and smiled; the simple words seemed so fitting, so like Augustine. *Ultimately you were a servus Dei,* thought Possidius. *You were a humble servant of God.*

"I think I have now, by God's help, discharged my obligation in writing this large work," wrote Augustine. "Let those who think I have said too little, or those who think I have said too much, forgive me; and let those who think I have said just enough join me in giving thanks to God. Amen."[8]

NOTES

Chapter One

1. Augustine, *Confessions & Enchiridion,* ed. and trans. Albert C. Outler (Philadelphia: Westminster Press, 1955), bk. 5, VIII, 15, in Christian Classics Ethereal Library [online] (cited 12 August 2002); available from http://www.ccel.org/a/augustine/confessions/confessions_enchiridion.txt.

Chapter Two

1. Augustine, *Confessions,* bk. 1, VII, 12.
2. Ibid., bk. 3, IV, 8.
3. Ibid., bk. 3, IV, 7.
4. Ibid., bk. 3, IV, 8.
5. Ibid.
6. Ibid., bk. 6, VIII, 13.

Chapter Three

1. Augustine, *Confessions,* bk. 5, VI, 11.
2. Ibid., bk. 5, VII, 12.
3. Ibid., bk. 9, III, 6.
4. Ibid., bk. 5, VI, 10.
5. Ibid., bk. 5, X, 18.

Chapter Four

1. Augustine, *Confessions,* bk. 5, XIII-XIV, 23–24.
2. Ibid., bk. 6, I, 1.
3. Ibid.
4. Ibid., bk. 6, XV, 25.

Chapter Five

1. Ambrose, *Saint Ambrose: Hexameron, Paradise, and Cain and Abel/Selected Works,* trans. John J. Savage, vol. 42 (New York: Fathers of the Church, Inc., 1961. Present copyright: Washington, D.C.: The Catholic Univ. of America Press), bk. I, chap.1–2.
2. Ambrose, *Hexameron,* bk. I, chap.1, 3–4.
3. Ibid., bk. I, chap. 2, 5 [Genesis 1:1 quoted in] .
4. Ibid., bk. I, chap. 8, 31.
5. Augustine, *Confessions,* bk. 6, XVI, 26.
6. Plotinus, "Concerning the Beautiful" (Paraphrase) in *Collected Writings of Plotinus,* trans. Thomas Taylor (Frome, Somerset, United Kingdom: The Prometheus Trust, 1994), I. vi. VI, 14.

7. Plotinus, "On the Nature and Origin of Evil" in *Collected Writings of Plotinus,* trans. Thomas Taylor (Frome, Somerset, United Kingdom: The Prometheus Trust, 1994), I. viii. XV, 99.

8. Augustine, *Confessions,* bk. 7, X, 16.

Chapter Six

1. Augustine, *Confessions,* bk. 6, VI,10.
2. Ibid., bk. 7, XXI, 27.
3. Ibid.
4. Ibid., bk. 8, II, 4.
5. Ibid.
6. Ibid., bk. 8, VI, 13.
7. Ibid., bk. 8, I, 1.
8. Ibid., bk. 8, I, 2.
9. Ibid., bk. 8, VII, 17.
10. Ibid., bk. 8, VI,15.
11. Ibid., bk. 8, VIII, 19.
12. Ibid., bk. 8, XI, 26.
13. Ibid., bk. 8, XI, 27.
14. Ibid., bk. 8, XII, 29.
15. Ibid. [Matthew 19:21 quoted in].
16. Ibid. [Romans 13:13-14 quoted in].
17. Ibid.
18. Ibid., bk. 8, IV, 9.

Chapter Seven

1. Augustine, *Confessions,* bk. 4, IV, 7.
2. Augustine, *Confessions,* bk. 4, IV, 8.
3. Ambrose, "The Sacraments" in *Saint Ambrose: Theological and Dogmatic Works,* trans. Roy J. Deferrari, vol. 44 (Washington, D.C.: Catholic Univ. of America Press, 1963), bk. II, chap. 7, 20, 286.
4. Augustine, *Confessions*, bk. 1, V, 6.

Chapter Eight

1. Ambrose, "The Mysteries" in *Saint Ambrose: Theological and Dogmatic Works,* trans. Roy J. Deferrari, vol. 44 (Washington, D.C.: Catholic Univ. of America Press, 1963), bk. I, chap. 1, 3, 6.
2. Augustine, *Confessions,* bk. 9, VI, 14.
3. Ibid.
4. Ambrose, "Book on the Mysteries," in *Saint Ambrose: Select Works and Letters,* ed. Philip Schaff and Henry Wace, series 2, vol. 10

(Grand Rapids, Mich.: William B. Eerdmans Publishing, 1890–1900), ch. VIII, 43, in Christian Classics Ethereal Library [online] (cited 12 August 2002); available from http://www.ccel.org/fathers2/NPNF2-10/Npnf2-10-29.htm#P6191_1583436.

5. Augustine, *Confessions,* bk. 9, X, 26.
6. Ibid., bk. 9, X, 24.
7. Ibid., bk. 9, X, 25.
8. Ibid., bk. 9, X, 26.
9. Ibid., bk. 9, XI, 27.
10. Ibid.
11. Ibid., bk. 9, XII, 32.
12. Ibid.
13. Ibid., bk. 9, XII, 33.

Chapter Nine
1. Augustine, *Confessions,* bk. 10, XXXIV, 51.
2. Ibid., bk. 9, VI, 14.
3. Ibid.
4. Augustine, *Prolegomena: Saint Augustine's Life and Work, Confessions, Letters,* ed. Philip Schaff, series 1, vol. 1 (Grand Rapids, Mich.: William B. Eerdmans Publishing, 1886–1890), letter VI, 1, in Christian Classics Ethereal Library [online] (cited 12 August 2002); available from http://www.ccel.org/fathers2/NPNF1-01/npnf1-01-22.htm#P2653_985633.

Chapter Ten
1. Augustine, "Acts or Disputation Against Fortunatus the Manichaean," in *Saint Augustine: Writings Against the Manichaeans and Against the Donatists,* ed. Philip Schaff, series 1, vol. 4 (Grand Rapids, Mich.: William B. Eerdmans Publishing, 1886–1890), "Disputation of the First Day," 1–2, in Christian Classics Ethereal Library [online] (cited 12 August 2002) available from http://www.ccel.org/fathers2/NPNF1-04/npnf1-04-09.htm#P818_430351
2. Ibid., "Disputation of the First Day," 14.
3. Ibid., "Disputation of the First Day, 19 [I Corinthians 15:50 quoted in].
4. Ibid., "Disputation of the First Day," 19.
5. Ibid., "Disputation of the Second Day," 19.
6. Ibid., "Disputation of the Second Day," 20.
7. Ibid.

8. Ibid.
9. Ibid.
10. Ibid., "Disputation of the Second Day," 21.
11. Ibid.
12. Ibid., "Disputation of the Second Day," 36–37.

Chapter Eleven
1. Augustine, *Prolegomena,* letter XXIX, 7.

Chapter Twelve
1. Augustine, *Confessions,* bk. 10, XXXVI, 59.
2. Ibid.
3. Augustine, "In Answer to the Letters of Petilian, the Donatist, Bishop of Cirta, in *Saint Augustine: Writings Against the Manichaeans and Against the Donatists,* ed. Philip Schaff, series 1, vol. 4 (Grand Rapids, Mich.: William B. Eerdmans Publishing, 1886–1890), bk. III, chap. 16, 38, in Christian Classics Ethereal Library [online] (cited 12 August 2002); available from http://www.ccel.org/fathers2/NPNF1-04/npnf1-04-59.htm #P4573_2288364.
4. Augustine, *Confessions,* bk. 11, I, 1 [Psalm 48:1 quoted in].
5. Ibid.
6. Ibid., bk. 10, XXVII, 38.
7. Augustine, "Augustine's Testimony Concerning the Confessions," in *Augustine: Confessions & Enchiridion,* ed. and trans. Albert C. Outler (Philadelphia: Westminster Press,1955) "Retractions," II, 6, 1, in Christian Classics Ethereal Library [online] (cited 12 August 2002); available from http://www.ccel.org/a/augustine/confessions/ confessions_enchiridion.txt.

Chapter Fourteen
1. Possidius, *Sancti Augustini vita. The Life of Saint Augustine,* ed. John Rotelle (Villanova, Penn.: Augustinian Press, 1988), xxii, 6–7.
2. Augustine, *Prolegomena,* letter LXXXIV, 1.
3. Augustine, *Sermon on the Mount, Harmony of the Gospels, Homilies on the Gospels,* ed. Philip Schaff, series 1, vol. 6 (Grand Rapids, Mich.: William B. Eerdmans Publishing, 1886–1890), sermon V, 1 [Matthew 5:22 quoted in], in Christian Classics Ethereal Library [online] (cited 12 August 2002); available from http://www.ccel.org/fathers2/ NPNF1-06/TOC.htm.
4. Ibid., sermon V, 2.

5. Ibid., sermon LV, 11.

Chapter Sixteen

1. Augustine, *Prolegomena,* letter CXXIV, 2.
2. Ibid., letter CXXXVI, 3.
3. Augustine, *The City of God and Christian Doctrine,* ed. Philip Schaff, series 1, vol. 2 (Grand Rapids, Mich.: William B. Eerdmans Publishing, 1886–1890), bk. IV, chap. 4, in Christian Classics Ethereal Library [online] (cited 12 August 2002); available from http://www.ccel.org/fathers2/NPNF1-02/TOC.htm.
4. Ibid., bk. IV, chap. 7.
5. Augustine, *Sermon on the Mount,* sermon LV, 9 [Luke 21:10 quoted in].
6. Ibid., sermon LV, 11.
7. Ibid., sermon LV, 9-10.
8. Augustine, *The City of God,* bk. XIV, chap. 1.
9. Ibid., bk. XIV, chap. 28.
10. Augustine, *Sermon on the Mount,* sermon XXXI, 8 [Psalm 103:5 quoted in].

Chapter Seventeen

1. Augustine, "On the Proceedings of Pelagius," in *Saint Augustine: Writings Against the Pelagians,* ed. Philip Schaff, series 1, vol. 5 (Grand Rapids, Mich.: William B. Eerdmans Publishing, 1886–1890), chap. 16, in Christian Classics Ethereal Library [online] (cited 12 August 2002); available from http://www.ccel.org/fathers2/NPNF1-05/TOC.htm.
2. Ibid.
3. Ibid., chap. 23.
4. Augustine, *Prolegomena,* letter CLXXXVIII, chap. 1, 2.
5. Ibid., letter CXCV.
6. Augustine, "A Treatise on the Grace of Christ and on Original Sin," in *Saint Augustine: Writings Against the Pelagians,* ed. Philip Schaff, series 1, vol. 5 (Grand Rapids, Mich.: William B. Eerdmans Publishing, 1886–1890), bk. I, chap. 2, in Christian Classics Ethereal Library [online] (cited 12 August 2002); available from http://www.ccel.org/fathers2/NPNF1-05/TOC.htm.
7. Ibid.
8. Augustine, *Prolegomena,* letter CXCII.
9. Ibid., letter CXCI, 2.

Chapter Eighteen

1. Augustine, *Prolegomena,* letter CCXI, 12.
2. Ibid., letter CCXI, 13.
3. Ibid., letter CCXIII, 1–2.
4. Ibid., letter CCXIII, 1.

Chapter Nineteen

1. Augustine, *The City of God,* bk. XXII, chap. 29.
2. Ibid.
3. Augustine, *Prolegomena,* letter CCXXVIII, 5.
4. Augustine, *The City of God,* bk. XXII, chap. 30.
5. Augustine, *Confessions,* bk. 10, XVII, 26.
6. Augustine, *The City of God,* bk., XXII, chap. 30.
7. Augustine, *Saint Augustine: Homilies on the Gospel of John, Homilies on the First Epistle of John, Soliloquies,* ed. Philip Schaff, series 1, vol. 7 (Grand Rapids, Mich.: William B. Eerdmans Publishing, 1886–1890), tractate XXVI, 4 [Psalm 37:4 quoted in], in Christian Classics Ethereal Library [online] (cited 12 August 2002); available from http://www.org/fathers2/NPNF1-07/TOC.htm.
8. Augustine, *The City of God,* bk. XXII, chap. 30.

SOURCES

Ambrose. *Saint Ambrose: Hexameron, Paradise, and Cain and Abel/Selected Works.* Trans. John J. Savage. The Fathers of the Church: A New Translation, vol. 42. New York: Fathers of the Church, Inc., 1961. Present copyright: Washington, D.C.: Catholic Univ. of America Press.

"Book on the Mysteries." In *Saint Ambrose: Select Works and Letters.* Ed. Philip Schaff. A Select Library of Nicene and Post-Nicene Fathers of the Christian Church, series 2, vol. 10. Grand Rapids, Mich.: William B. Eerdmans Publishing, 1896. In Christian Classics Ethereal Library [online]. Grand Rapids, Mich. [cited 12 August 2002]. Available from http://www.ccel.org/fathers2/NPNF2-10/ TOC.htm.

"The Mysteries." In *Saint Ambrose: Theological and Dogmatic Works.* Trans. Roy J. Deferrari. The Fathers of the Church: A New Translation, vol. 44. Washington, D.C.: Catholic Univ. of America Press, 1963.

"The Sacraments." In *Saint Ambrose: Theological and Dogmatic Works.* Trans. Roy J. Deferrari. The Fathers of the Church: A New Translation, vol. 44. Washington, D.C.: Catholic Univ. of America Press, 1963.

Augustine, Aurelius. "Acts or Disputation Against Fortunatus, the Manichaean." In *Saint Augustine: The Writings Against the Manichaeans and Against the Donatists.* Ed. Philip Schaff. A Select Library of the Nicene and Post-Nicene Fathers of the Christian Church, series 1, vol. 4. Grand Rapids, Mich.: William B. Eerdmans Publishing, 1886–1890. In Christian Classics Ethereal Library [online]. Grand Rapids, Mich. [cited 12 August 2002]. Available from http://www.ccel.org/fathers2/NPNF1-04/TOC.htm.

Augustine, *Confessions & Enchiridion.* Ed. and trans. Albert C. Outler. Philadelphia: Westminster Press,1955. In Christian Classics Ethereal Library [online]. Grand Rapids, Mich. [cited 12 August 2002]. Available from http://www.ccel.org/a/augustine/confessions/confessions_enchiridion.txt.

"Augustine's Testimony Concerning the Confessions." In *Confessions and Enchiridion.* Ed. and trans. Albert C. Outler. Philadelphia: Westminster Press,1955. In Christian Classics Ethereal Library [online]. Grand Rapids, Mich. [cited 12 August 2002]. Available from http://www.ccel.org/a/augustine/confessions/confessions_enchiridion.txt.

Saint Augustine's City of God and Christian Doctrine. Ed. Philip
Schaff. A Select Library of the Nicene and Post-Nicene Fathers of the
Christian Church, series 1, vol. 2. Grand Rapids, Mich.: William B.
Eerdmans Publishing, 1886–1890. In Christian Classics Ethereal
Library [online]. Grand Rapids, Mich. [cited 12 August 2002].
Available from http://www.ccel.org/fathers2/NPNF1-02/TOC.htm.

*Homilies on the Gospel of John, Homilies on the First Epistle of John,
Soliloquies.* Ed. Philip Schaff. A Select Library of the Nicene and
Post-Nicene Fathers of the Christian Church, series 1, vol. 7. Grand
Rapids, Mich.: William B. Eerdmans Publishing, 1886–1890. In
Christian Classics Ethereal Library [online]. Grand Rapids, Mich.
[cited 12 August 2002]. Available from http://www.org/fathers2/
NPNF1-07/TOC.htm.

"In Answer to the Letters of Petilian, the Donatist, Bishop of Cirta."
In *Saint Augustine: The Writings Against the Manichaeans and
Against the Donatists.* Ed. Philip Schaff. A Select Library of the
Nicene and Post-Nicene Fathers of the Christian Church, series 1,
vol. 4. Grand Rapids, Mich.: William B. Eerdmans
Publishing,1886–1890. In Christian Classics Ethereal Library
[online]. Grand Rapids, Mich. [cited 12 August 2002]. Available
from http://www.ccel.org/fathers2/NPNF1-04/TOC.htm.

"Letters of Saint Augustine." In *Prolegomena: Saint Augustine's Life
and Work; Confessions; and Letters.* Ed. Philip Schaff. A Select
Library of the Nicene and Post-Nicene Fathers of the Christian
Church, series 1, vol. 1. Grand Rapids, Mich.: William B.
Eerdmans Publishing,1886–1890. In Christian Classics Ethereal
Library [online]. Grand Rapids, Mich. [cited 12 August 2002].
Available from http://www.ccel.org/fathers2/NPNF1-01/TOC.htm.

"On the Proceedings of Pelagius." In *Saint Augustine: Anti-Pelagian
Writings.* Ed. Philip Schaff. A Select Library of the Nicene
and Post-Nicene Fathers of the Christian Church, series 1,
vol. 5. Grand Rapids, Mich.: William B. Eerdmans Publishing,
1886–1890. In Christian Classics Ethereal Library [online].
Grand Rapids, Mich. [cited 12 August 2002]. Available from
http://www.ccel.org/fathers2/NPNF1-05/TOC.htm.

*Sermon on the Mount, Harmony of the Gospels, Homilies on
the Gospels.* Ed. Philip Schaff. A Select Library of the Nicene
and Post-Nicene Fathers of the Christian Church, series 1,
vol. 6. Grand Rapids, Mich.: William B. Eerdmans Publishing,
1886–1890. In Christian Classics Ethereal Library [online].

Grand Rapids, Mich. [cited 12 August 2002]. Available from http://www.ccel.org/fathers2/NPNF1-06/TOC.htm.

"A Treatise on the Grace of Christ and on Original Sin." In *Saint Augustin: Anti-Pelagian Writings*. Ed. Philip Schaff. A Select Library of the Nicene and Post-Nicene Fathers of the Christian Church, series 1, vol. 5. Grand Rapids, Mich.: William B. Eerdmans Publishing, 1886–1890. In Christian Classics Ethereal Library [online]. Grand Rapids, Mich. [cited 12 August 2002]. Available from http://www.ccel.org/fathers2/NPNF1-05/TOC.htm.

"Venatio I." [online]. Brooklyn, N.Y. [cited 23 May 2002]. Available from http://depthome.brooklyn. cuny.edu/classics/gladiatr/ venatio1.htm.

Brown, Peter. *Augustine of Hippo*. London: Univ. of California Press, 2000.

Dunkle, Roger. Brooklyn College Classics Department Home Page. "The Experience." [online]. Brooklyn, N. Y. [cited 23 May 2002]. Available from http://depthome.brooklyn.cuny.edu/classics/ gladiatr/arena.htm.

Fitzgerald, Allan, ed. *Augustine Through the Ages: An Encyclopedia*. Grand Rapids, Mich.: William B. Eerdmans Publishing Company, 1999.

Imber, Margaret. "The Gladiator." Bates College [online]. Lewiston, Maine [cited 23 May 2002]. Available from http://abacus.bates.edu/ ~mimber/Rciv/gladiator.prof.htm.

Plotinus. "Concerning the Beautiful" (Paraphrase). In *Collected Writings of Plotinus*. Trans. Thomas Taylor. Frome, Somerset, United Kingdom: Prometheus Trust, 1994.

"On the Nature and Origin of Evil." In *Collected Writings of Plotinus*. Trans. Thomas Taylor. Frome, Somerset, United Kingdom: Prometheus Trust, 1994.

Possidius. *Sancti Augustini vita. The Life of Saint Augustine*. Ed. John Rotelle. Villanova, Penn.: Augustinian Press, 1988.

Tilley, Maureen. *Donatist Martyr Stories: The Church in Conflict in Roman North Africa*. Liverpool, England: Liverpool Univ. Press, 1996.

Wills, Garry. *Saint Augustine*. New York: Viking (Penguin Group), 1999.

HEROES OF THE FAITH

This exciting biographical series explores the lives of famous Christian men and women throughout the ages. These trade paper books will inspire and encourage you to follow the example of these "Heroes of the Faith" who made Christ the center of their existence. 208 pages each. Only $3.97 each!

Brother Andrew, God's Undercover Agent

Gladys Aylward, Missionary to China

Dietrich Bonhoeffer, Opponent of the Nazi Regime

Corrie ten Boom, Heroine of Haarlem

William and Catherine Booth, Founders of the Salvation Army

John Bunyan, Author of *The Pilgrim's Progress*

John Calvin, Father of Reformed Theology

William Carey, Father of Missions

Amy Carmichael, Abandoned to God

George Washington Carver, Inventor and Naturalist

Fanny Crosby, the Hymn Writer

Frederick Douglass, Abolitionist and Reformer

Jonathan Edwards, the Great Awakener

Jim Elliot, Missionary to Ecuador

Charles Finney, the Great Revivalist

Billy Graham, the Great Evangelist

C. S. Lewis, Author of *Mere Christianity*

Eric Liddell, Olympian and Missionary

David Livingstone, Missionary and Explorer

Martin Luther, the Great Reformer

D. L. Moody, the American Evangelist

Samuel Morris, the Apostle of Simple Faith

George Müller, Man of Faith

Mother Teresa, Missionary of Charity

Watchman Nee, Man of Suffering

John Newton, Author of "Amazing Grace"

Florence Nightingale, Lady with the Lamp

Luis Palau, Evangelist to the World

Francis and Edith Schaeffer, Defenders of the Faith

Charles Sheldon, Author of *In His Steps*

Mary Slessor, Queen of Calabar

Charles Spurgeon, the Great Orator

John and Betty Stam, Missionary Martyrs

Billy Sunday, Evangelist on Sawdust Trail

Hudson Taylor, Founder, China Inland Mission

Sojourner Truth, American Abolitionist

William Tyndale, Bible Translator and Martyr

John Wesley, the Great Methodist

George Whitefield, Pioneering Evangelist

William Wilberforce, Abolitionist, Politician, Writer

John Wycliffe, Herald of the Reformation

Available wherever books are sold.
Or order from:
Barbour Publishing, Inc.
P.O. Box 719
Uhrichsville, Ohio 44683
www.barbourbooks.com

If you order by mail, add $2.00 to your order for shipping.
Prices subject to change without notice.